THE ARTHUR AVENUE COOKBOOK

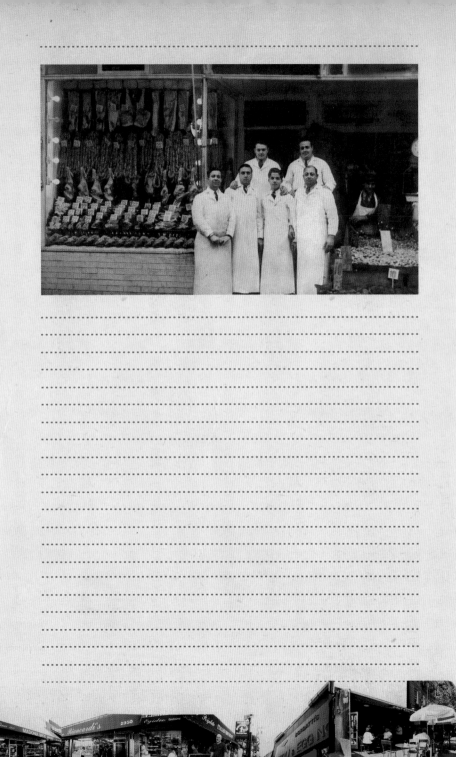

THE ARTHUR AVENUE COOKBOOK

RECIPES AND MEMORIES FROM THE REAL LITTLE ITALY

ANN VOLKWEIN

Photographs by *Vegar Abelsnes*

10 ReganBooks
Celebrating Ten Bestselling Years
An Imprint of HarperCollinsPublishers

FIRST EDITION

Designed by HSU+ASSOCIATES

PRINTED ON ACID-FREE PAPER
LIBRARY OF CONGRESS CATALOGING-IN-PUBLICATION DATA
Volkwein, Ann.
The Arthur Avenue cookbook : recipes and memories from the real Little Italy / Ann
Volkwein ; photographs by Vegar Abelsnes. — 1st ed.
p. cm. Includes index.
ISBN 0-06-056715-5
1. Cookery, Italian. 2. Bronx (New York, N.Y.) I. Title.

TX723.V587 2004
641.5945—dc22   2004041784
04 05 06 07 08 ❖/TP 10 9 8 7 6 5 4 3 2 1

FOR ALL THE FAMILIES

WHO RETURN HOME TO ARTHUR AVENUE

Joe Liberatore displays a picture of his brother, circa 1936

CONTENTS

Borgatti's Ravioli and Egg Noodles,
circa 1947

Panini piled high at Mike's Deli

ACKNOWLEDGMENTS

It takes a village, in this case a neighborhood, to accomplish this type of project. Belmont-born Betty-Ann Iannaccio and Paul Bloom provided my introduction to David Greco of Mike's Deli, whose devotion to the neighborhood and its future is extraordinary. Over the course of the past year and a half David encouraged and cajoled—even did some food styling and gave me personal introductions to his fellow shop and restaurant owners. Among the many who warmly embraced my efforts and generously shared their personal histories and recipes were Laurence Addeo (Junior and Senior), Anthony Artuso (Junior and Senior), Sal Biancardi, Chris and Mario Borgatti, Mike Rella, Peter Servedio, Frank Randazzo, Charlie Lalima, Peter DeLuca, and Roberto Paciullo. This is their book. Special thanks as well to Arthur Avenue–native Frank Franz of the Belmont Small Business Association and the staff of the Enrico Fermi Cultural Center.

Many thanks to my agent, John Michel, for his wisdom and well-timed cheerleading techniques, to Katherine Constable for bolstering my spirits and tirelessly transcribing, to Leslie Orlandini for her expert baking and recipe tweaking, and to Shirley Fan, Simon Constable, and Lindley Kirksey for their enthusiastic testing and tasting. Thanks also to Georgia Downard for her mentorship.

Judith Regan's great vision made *The Arthur Avenue Cookbook* a reality. It was a gift to write this book and to get to know these wonderful families. I am grateful to her for the opportunity to work on a project that has such meaning to me and that touches so many lives. Many thanks as well to my editor, Aliza Fogelson, for her unwavering support (in the face of an extremely complex manuscript delivery), and her thoughtful direction throughout the duration of the project.

Finally, to the ever-patient and marvelously talented Vegar Abelsnes, whose beautiful, dignified photographs capture Arthur Avenue in ways words and recipes alone could not accomplish. Thank you for your friendship and partnership.

FOREWORD

Arthur Avenue is indisputably Italian, and indisputably American. Whenever I visit, I'm struck by the fact that it's a little out of kilter with the rest of New York City—which is one of the reasons I like to go there. Arthur Avenue still has a very live and living Italian street market just like you'd find in many regular medium-sized cities in Italy. The food merchants line several blocks, and there's a sense of community and a sense of favoritism; every grandma has her favorite place to get her meat and her artichokes.

Part of the romance of Arthur Avenue, which this book captures so well, is that it is timeless and touched by the immigrants who first settled there, and at the same time modern. We filmed several episodes of *Ciao America* up on Arthur Avenue last summer, and I remember thinking after the second visit that it was like a little neighborhood in Naples: Every café owner, every cop, every fireman, every person on the street knows each other, and they all say hello to you and everyone wants to have a coffee with you and welcome you. Now, it's not only the grandmas who shop on Arthur Avenue—it's their sons and daughters and grandchildren, and everyone's cooking, and Arthur Avenue is still a very vibrant part of the Italian culture. And while the neighborhood has (refreshingly) not changed very much over the ten years I've been going there—and apparently, the decades before that—it has begun to draw in a wider circle, including the yuppie foodies and tourists and others who visit looking for an authentic and realistic experience. Magically, these new visitors haven't changed the timbre of the place or the tone of the people or the way stores operate. Arthur Avenue is still geared toward the Italian locals, still has the mom and pop shops that could make more money if they stayed open longer or if they wanted to be more aggressive about advertising. Instead, the people of Arthur Avenue are happy to continue to sell their fresh pasta and their deli products as they always have. They preserve a sense of old Italian charm that way. Biancardi's Meats is wonderful, and David Greco of Mike's Deli is a relic who is individually responsible for maintaining and promoting a lot of the character of the neighborhood. When I'm going to make a special Italian meal for my family, I shop on Arthur Avenue.

There's no longer a need to worry about time changing Arthur Avenue, and no need to miss out on it for those who live far from New York. *The Arthur Avenue Cookbook* beautifully preserves an intact Italian experience that has yet to lose its tanginess, its particular flavor that makes it feel really familial, really familiar, and really expressive of the Italian spirit.

Mario Batali April 2004

THE ARTHUR AVENUE COOKBOOK

Intoxicating aromas *flow from the transom windows of* *Addeo Bakers,* *shoppers pause at* *Randazzo's oyster* *cart for a quick dozen,* *Joe Liberatore* *tenderly handles a small pot of basil at the entrance to the indoor market, and from behind his deli counter* *Mike Greco* *greets the ladies with a mischievous wink while belting out an aria.*

O n Arthur Avenue, the Little Italy of the Bronx, these are everyday sights and sounds and smells, versions of which have been played out daily on these streets for almost a hundred years. "It's an enigma; it is without a doubt an enigma!" exclaims Sal Biancardi of Biancardi Meats. "I've said this before and I say I defy anyone to find this number of businesses concentrated within a three-block area that are still run by the same families that ran them sixty years ago. We haven't really lost any big names. They stood the test of time. Not an easy thing to do to pass businesses from generation to generation. Especially *these* kinds of businesses in today's day and age."

This Bronx tale, the story of a neighborhood, started at the turn of the century when Italian immigrants began to pass through Ellis Island in large numbers and settle in the boroughs of New York City. Belmont, as the wider area is known, was once home to over

fifty-thousand Italian immigrants, living in tenements and houses that stretched from Southern Boulevard to Third Avenue and from Fordham Road down to 183rd Street. Today, the natural boundaries of the neighborhood are the Bronx Zoo, which borders Southern Boulevard along the eastern edge, the Botanical Garden to the northeast, Fordham University to the north, St. Barnabas Hospital to the west, and 183rd Street to the south.

Arthur Avenue and 187th Street form the crossroads of the neighborhood, and the shops and restaurants are huddled together in a triangular cluster from 183rd to 188th and along East 187th Street to Beaumont Avenue. Among the variety of stores are two fish markets, four butchers, two pork stores, four pastry shops, five gourmet delis, six bread stores, two cheese shops, one pasta shop, and more than a dozen restaurants.

A tour of the community, whether in person or through the profiles and recipes in this book, reveals that those who run businesses here, as their fathers did and in many cases their grandfathers did, are dedicated not only to their own shops or restaurants but to the culture of the neighborhood. Arthur Avenue is a unique, living memorial to the labors and determination of a vital community of Italian-American immigrants.

The American dream has been replayed thousands of times in Belmont. Families work hard, move to the nearby suburbs of Throgs Neck or Pelham, then on to more upscale Westchester towns, or out to Long Island. Over the years, the neighborhood has changed as the immi-gration flow has shifted away from Italians to Albanians and Mexicans. It's the same story retold in many New York neighborhoods, but what sets Arthur Avenue apart, what makes it an "enigma," is the number of Italian-American shop and restaurant owners who have remained, and the droves of former residents who return consistently, week after week or on holidays, from miles and miles away. For some shop owners it's the strength of their family values and pride in their family name that keeps them here, for others it's the returning customers, the relationships that cut across generations. For the Italian-American shoppers it's a most unusual trip down memory lane—complete with full-sensory envelopment, and the promise of high quality and great value. Beyond that customer base, however, Arthur Avenue serves its new community well, as Sal Biancardi points out: Albanians have "the same sort of European shopping needs as Italians, so they fit in perfectly." And the cycle has begun for Albanians, as Sal notes, "now they're moving out but they come back and shop [just as the Italians do]."

The Mexican population may not share the same European shopping needs, but they do share the Catholic faith with the Italians and Albanians of the neighborhood, support Our Lady of Mount Carmel, and work in the shops and restaurants. Arthur Avenue's role in history seems to be as incubator for new Americans, an extended Italian-American family forever nurturing first-generation sons and daughters, feeding memories as well as stomachs along the way.

OUR LADY OF MOUNT CARMEL
187th Street between Hughes and Belmont Avenues

Votive candles, Our Lady of Mount Carmel

Nobly gracing 187th Street at the corner of Belmont, the church has been the architectural and cultural anchor of the neighborhood from the time it was built. At the turn of the century, Italians in the neighborhood attended church up on the Grand Concourse, and by 1906 their numbers had grown so strong that the monsignor started a parish in a storefront at 659 East 187th Street. Father Joseph Caffuzzi celebrated the first mass. In 1907 they broke ground on the lower part of the church and in 1917 the upper section was begun on what became Our Lady of Mount Carmel.

"Our Lady of Mount Carmel was built on the backs of Italian immigrants," says Jerry Galliano of Arthur Avenue Bread. He means that quite literally: the community donated the funds, but also much of the labor. Many of the parishioners worked in construction, building the Bronx Zoo, the Botanical Garden, and the city's transit systems. "In New York City the church is basically Irish so they wanted their own voice; they wanted to say, 'We're Italian. Our Lady of Mount Carmel is going to be our mother; she is going to be the one we praise in our services.' Same with St. Anthony. So you notice we have the Feast

of St. Anthony and we have the Feast of Our Lady of Mount Carmel. The church was the backbone of this community and I believe it still is. You will see at holidays Italians from all over the tristate area who used to live here come back for Easter services. We go every day but we can't get in at Easter because it's packed. Wherever you go you always come back home. So many people have been gone away forty years yet their children still get married there. The church speaks for itself; outside it's Romanesque but inside it's like a Renaissance palace."

Mario Borgatti, of Borgatti's Ravioli & Egg Noodles, shares some memories of the church's heyday: "It's safe to say we used to have ten to twelve masses here on Sunday starting at six A.M., several in Italian, maybe two, three, four, at a time. As an altar boy here I served mass every morning. I had a friend in my class at school and we'd be here at six o'clock to serve mass, then we'd go to school after that. There were so many people going there that at times as an usher we would serve eleven hundred people at one mass. There were so many kids at the nine A.M. mass that the adults were not allowed there, they had to go down to the lower church. Today it's a struggle to get eleven hundred at all the masses combined."

Nonetheless, the church continues to have two masses a day in Italian, although many of the parishioners are Spanish-speaking or Albanian. The feasts are well attended each June and July, and the abundance of glowing votive candles alone is proof of an active parish. Across the street is a Catholic Goods Center, replete with statues of saints, Bibles, funeral memorials, even religious cookbooks. On Saturdays you'll find proprietor and Arthur Avenue native John Iazzetti, Jr., standing in the doorway, perhaps speaking Italian to a nun from the church. He's only the third owner in the shop's eighty-year history. John's mother's grandfather came to live on Arthur Avenue in 1886. His father also grew up on Arthur Avenue and became a bartender and pizza maker for Mario's Restaurant. He says, "Growing up, we never left the neighborhood. There was no need to; there were schools, jobs. It functioned like a small town in Italy. A lot

of things revolved around the church. Sundays people were strolling down the street; it was not unusual to see men walking arm in arm. Everybody in the building was Italian." The Iazzettis are a good example of the tight-knit families from the neighborhood. John has six brothers and sisters and claims, "Every last one of them knows how to cook. That stems from the kitchen being the center of activity; we had a large eat-in kitchen." He shares an anecdote about cooking while handing over a prayer card. "That's St. Laurentius, the saint of cooks. He's always portrayed holding a grill because the Romans grilled him to death. And you know what his last words were? 'Turn me over; I'm done.'" John breaks out into a wide grin exclaiming, "Now that's a Christian!"

John Iazzetti outside his Catholic Goods Center

Arthur Avenue Retail Market
2344 Arthur Avenue

By the late 1930s Arthur Avenue supported a sea of pushcart vendors selling their wares on the street in sweltering heat and bitter cold. In response to their hardship, Mayor Fiorello La Guardia championed the construction of what became the commercial heart of the area, the Arthur Avenue Retail Market. The market opened in 1940, providing six by eight-foot stalls for the vendors under its skylit roof. Step in off the Avenue today and you meet Joe Liberatore, a former pushcart owner and one of the original retailers at the market. Tucked in around his selection of produce, seeds, and plants is a collection of photographs that provide a snapshot of New York history, from the framed photo of his brother John in front of the pushcart around 1936, to Joe greeting Mayor La Guardia, Terence Cardinal Cooke, former mayor Rudolph Giuliani—even Senator Hillary Rodham Clinton. Joe is certainly the "mayor" of the market, but its current president is Mike Rella of Peter's Meat Market. As I chatted with Mike over a cappuccino, he related how the market, along with the neighborhood itself, experienced a downturn in the 1970s. The market was losing money and the city no longer wanted to manage it, so the vendors formed a volunteer association. Former housewares merchant Isidore Berenstein served as president of the cooperative from 1970 until 1995,

TOP LEFT AND FOLLOWING PAGES: Cigar rolling at La Casa Grande inside the market
ABOVE: Mike and Dave Greco serve up prosciutto
OPPOSITE: Mike Greco holds court behind his deli counter

when Mike took over. "We have eighteen merchants here, and when you have eighteen people under one roof you're going to have a problem here and there but it can be fixed. We get together, we talk about it, what to do to make the customers happy, because if I upset a customer, everybody loses. A customer comes here for a piece of steak and they see a great cheese hanging there, they're gonna buy that cheese."

When the market opened, each stall specialized in one thing (you wanted potatoes, you went to the potato man, tomatoes, over to the man behind the pyramid of tomatoes), and it's still an unwritten rule that vendors not compete within the market. For example, Mario's Meat Specialties sells organ meats exclusively; Peter's Meat Market sells all cuts of meat other than organ meat but doesn't sell cold cuts because their neighbor, Mike's Deli, does. The market today still boasts produce stands,

but you'll also find café tables, La Casa Grande—a business devoted to hand-rolled cigars—a rotisserie, a bakery, a housewares merchant, and of course Mike's Deli with its garland of dried sausages, buckets of olives, and colorful piles of panini. It's a unique atmosphere, lovingly looked after by the vendors. Mike Rella of Peter's Meat Market says, "I've been here since 1967. There's so much history in this market it's unbelievable. I remember good times; I remember bad times. I remember when no one wanted to come into this market because they said it was rundown." The renaissance of the market in the early eighties, through the hard work of the association, helped the economic resurgence of the entire neighborhood, and it thrives as a draw for returning former residents, shopping bags in hand.

THE ARTHUR AVENUE COOKBOOK ANN VOLKWEIN

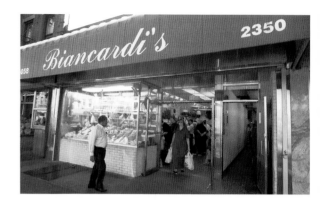

Recipes and Memories

Beyond the riches of the restaurants, the delights of Arthur Avenue, from the meats to the fish to the fresh mozzarella and rounds of bread, come into full glory in the kitchens of those who shop and work here. Neighborhood shop and restaurant owners provided the recipes in the following pages, generously sharing the flavors of their family tables. While there is an overwhelming preponderance of southern Italian heritage on the avenue, Sal Biancardi makes the observation that a family's original roots cannot strictly define their style of cooking.

"This is not Italian cooking here, this is influenced by Italian cooking but has become something else. Like everything else it has evolved into something of its own. We make dried sausage that you can trace back to Neapolitan roots but it is very different from the dried sausage that you find in Naples today. Why?" Sal proposes, "Because it had to adapt to the way the Italian-American culture had changed. They don't want to give up those roots but you know the sausage had to become leaner. It changes, so again it's like everything else around here. It's Italian-American not Italian. It's like if you took Italians and stuck them over here for a while, what would happen? If you look at the same town in Italy and what they were producing sixty years ago they're probably not much different, whereas things have changed here dramatically. They've adapted to different cultures. They've managed to hold on to their roots but they've adapted through

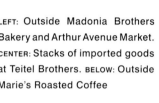

OPPOSITE PAGE RIGHT: Biancardi's Meats. Laurence, Salvatore, and Laura Addeo, circa 1934

LEFT: Outside Madonia Brothers Bakery and Arthur Avenue Market. CENTER: Stacks of imported goods at Teitel Brothers. BELOW: Outside Marie's Roasted Coffee

generations. It's a function of nature; it's a function of human nature."

Surviving the process of time and adaptation, family histories are etched on the storefronts of Arthur Avenue. Laurence Addeo Jr., a third-generation owner of Addeo Bakers, recognizes his role in preserving the memories, "I was born but not raised in the Bronx. My father's generation was really the last generation to grow up here . . . I took a class on storytelling in college, and even though I didn't grow up here I'll be telling all the stories because they were told to me. You gotta hope that that kind of thing goes on."

The story of this neighborhood begins and ends with the Italian-American families that strive every day to keep it alive and thriving as New York's real Little Italy. Savor the stories and the memories, the recipes and tips from some of Arthur Avenue's greatest families.

Buon appetito.

RECIPES

Antipasti

Profiles:

**Mike's Deli
and Arthur Avenue Cafè and Caterers**

Teitel Brothers

Mike's Deli and Arthur Avenue Caterers
david and his father, michele "pops" greco

Profile
2344 Arthur Avenue
Bronx, NY 10458
718-295-5033
www.arthuravenue.com

Come here for antipasti, prosciutto, sopressata, mort-adella, house-smoked mozzarella, imported cheese, olives—the list goes on. They also make superb deli sandwiches, and their café tables afford some of the best people-watching in the neighborhood. Mike's son David Greco has expanded the business into catering, and also ships their products to customers with cravings.

SIMPLY PUT, Michele "Pops" Greco is a force of nature. He holds court behind his deli counter, equal parts ringmaster and Rudolph Valentino, with a little Mussolini thrown in. On any given Saturday he's belting out *Rigoletto,* offering a sip of wine to a customer, and, famously, flirting with the ladies with his robust accent and prancing blue eyes.

Mike was born in Calabria in 1929. His father had been frequenting the United States since 1895, working for forty years in the bar business but never settling in this country as Mike's mother didn't want to immigrate permanently. "Every time he'd go back [to Italy] he'd create a bambino and come back," jokes Mike. At about age eighteen Mike fell in love with a local girl that his parents didn't approve of. "I used to say to my father I want to marry her because I want to go to America. He said, 'You want to go to America,

ABOVE: Michele and David Greco, father and son, have made Mike's Deli an institution.

don't worry about it I send you to America.' Three days later, me and my twin brother, he brings us to the council in Naples… and a few months later we come to this country… on a Russian boat, the *Sobieski.*"

That was 1947. By 1948, Mike started working in a butcher shop on Arthur Avenue owned by the Cappiello family. Gennaro (aka "the redheaded butcher from Naples") and Louisa Cappiello had been doing business on the Avenue since 1919. They had a daughter named Antoinette and it didn't take long for the charming Calabrese to fall in love with her. By 1951, they were married. Eager to do something on his own, Mike started working at the deli in his current location in 1955 and by 1969 the final deal was sealed. Mike's Deli was born. By this time Mike and Antoinette had had four children, Louisa, Anna Maria, David, and Marco.

After their divorce in 1971, Mike says he "went broke," but with some divine intervention and a little help from his brother Joe he was able to get on his feet. As Mike tells it, he was on the brink of losing his deli when he had a dream in which Pope John II came to him, patted him on the shoulder, and said "Everything's going to be all right, go to sleep." The next day his brother, by then a successful restaurateur, called and said, "I'm going to send you a customer from Las Vegas, he's a nice customer, take care of him." As the story goes, this guy showed up two days later and ended up spending $3,000. Then Mike walks outside and sees an old man with white hair, who asks, "You want to play a number?" Not being a numbers player, he hesitated but decided to take a chance… and made out with enough to save his business.

"That's when everything started up. The life started to roll more easy," Mike remembers. "My sons and daughters, they started to get big and they started working for me. Louisa and Anna Maria, they were very good behind the counter. Marco, he was very good with the mozzarella. It just got better and better, we got a good reputation… And then my son [Dave] now, he does well, he got a lotta nice people. He knows what he's doing. You know my policy that I teach to my sons and daughters: 'What you eat the customer is gonna eat. And what you don't like is no good for my customer. My customer is the important thing.'"

Mike has noted all the changes in the neighborhood over the years, for better or for worse. "I remember when 'the boys' were here, 1948 to 1970, the neighborhood was in better shape . . . Every time you wanted to start a business you had to go through them to find out whether it was good or bad. They were looking out for the neighborhood," Mike explains. "The neighborhood started to change in the 1970s because the big fish came in and the big fish they think differently than the small fish. The big ones they have a different kind of mentality. . . . Many years ago you used to go in the neighborhood and knock on the door. 'Hey, you prepared the gravy?' Everything was open; it was beautiful."

Times have changed but that doesn't mean that Mike wants to be anywhere but on the Avenue. He's refused dozens of offers to open businesses elsewhere; his loyalty to

LEFT: A view from behind the deli counter; an employee sports a T-shirt printed with a famous quote from "Pops." RIGHT: Mike Greco pours a glass of vino for a customer.

ABOVE: An early photo of the deli with Michele in the middle.

his customers is steadfast, and it's their return visits for years and over generations that keeps him going. Dave Greco has taken over for his father now but Mike refuses to retire, insisting, "I don't want to die." His brother Joe died a year after he left his restaurant, JoeNina's, over on Westchester Avenue. JoeNina's had legendary status in the Bronx. Everybody who was anybody ate there, top doctors, lawyers—even John Gotti in his heyday. Joe was ahead of his time, a perfectionist who would have his purveyor, Joe "Bananas," order twenty cases of tomatoes, then hand pick five cases worthy of delivery. The meticulous chef-restaurateur would set them on a shelf and watch them ripen before plucking them right at their peak. Everything was cooked to order, none of this "slop and shop" as Dave puts it. "I spent as much time as I could handle with my father and my uncle," he says, crediting the two of them and his grandmother Maria for his culinary secrets. If his father was Mussolini his uncle was "junior Mussolini," laughs David, "one crazy Calabrese."

David works hard to strengthen the community of shop owners on the Avenue, with an eye toward the future and aspirations that include a cooking show. The care he gives his business and his customers is directly related to his father's dedicated instruction: "It wasn't just a lesson about salami and cheese; it was a lesson about life that revolved around salami and cheese." David reflects a moment then adds with a grin, "And there was usually a woman involved, too."

Fair warning to all female customers, Mike can make the phrase "taste my mozzarella" sound like a proposal, and his passion is so great he sheds tears while reminiscing. In the end, his deli is his Trevi Fountain, and as he's fond of saying, "All the world's a stage, and this is *my* stage."

ANTIPASTI PLATE

MAKES 4 (HEALTHY) SERVINGS

From:

Mike's Deli and Arthur Avenue Café

david and his father, michele "pops" greco

Ingredients:

6 ounces prosciutto di Parma, thinly sliced

6 ounces mortadella

1 sopressata (6 ounces), skinned and thinly sliced

1 homemade (6 ounces), dried, sweet Italian sausage, thinly sliced

1 homemade (6 ounces), dried, hot Italian sausage, thinly sliced

1/2 pound sharp imported provolone, sliced into 1 x 1/2-inch batons

1/2 pound Parmigiano-Reggiano, cut into chunks

1/2 pound Calabrese peppered pecorino

1/4 pound fresh mozzarella, sliced 1/4 to 1/2 inch thick

1 tomato, sliced

Salt and pepper to taste

Extra-virgin olive oil to drizzle

Basil leaves to garnish

Directions:

Prepare a large platter with listed ingredients. For presentation, David rolls each slice of the prosciutto, mortadella, and sopressata and fans them around the edge of the plate, alternating with sections of the sausages, provolone, Parmigiano-Reggiano, and pecorino. Serve the mozzarella alongside the slices of tomato. Salt and pepper the platter, then drizzle with the extra-virgin olive oil. Garnish with basil leaves.

Serve this colorful platter of meat and cheese alongside a basket of crusty Pane di Casa (page 142).

GRILLED AND MARINATED VEGETABLE PLATTER

MAKES 4 (HEALTHY) SERVINGS

From:

Mike's Deli and Arthur Avenue Café

david and his father, michele "pops" greco

Ingredients:

1 small eggplant, very thinly sliced, skin-on
Salt to taste
2 large carrots, very thinly sliced
1 medium zucchini, very thinly sliced
Pepper to taste
2 cups extra-virgin olive oil
4 garlic cloves, minced
6 medium portobello mushrooms, stems trimmed off
1 yellow bell pepper
1 red bell pepper
1 green bell pepper
$^1/_2$ pound sun-dried tomatoes
1 cup mixed olives
Reduced balsamic vinegar
  (simmer 1 to 2 cups until reduced by half)

David uses a slicing machine when preparing the eggplant, zucchini, and carrots; the key is to cut them as thinly as possible, less than a quarter inch thick.

Directions:

Heat a grill pan over high heat or set a grill to high (you can also use a broiler). Preheat the oven to 400° F. On the stove top, bring a pot of water to boil for parboiling and blanching.

Lightly salt the eggplant. Place the carrot slices in the pot of boiling water and parboil them for about 1 minute, remove and pat dry. Brush the eggplant, zucchini, and carrots with some of the olive oil. Grill these vegetables, in batches, for about 1 or 2 minutes per side, or until grill-marks are apparent. Remove them to a roasting pan and finish cooking them in the oven, about 3 to 7 minutes (depending on the vegetable); until flexible but not mushy. When done, salt and pepper them, drizzle with some of the olive oil and set aside.

Mix the garlic with 2 tablespoons of the remaining olive oil. Spread the mixture on the well of each of the mushrooms. Bake them in the oven for 10 to 15 minutes, or until softened. Remove from the oven and finish them on the grill, about a minute, turning once. Season with salt and pepper, slice the mushrooms into $^1/_4$- to $^1/_2$-inch wide strips, and set aside.

Over an open flame or under a broiler, roast the peppers, turning when necessary, until their skin is charred and blackened. Hold them under cold water and peel off the skin. Pat them dry. Seed and slice them into $^1/_2$-inch wide strips. Drizzle them with more of the olive oil, season with salt and pepper, and set aside.

Blanch the sun-dried tomatoes in the boiling water for 1 to 2 minutes. Remove and pat dry. Coat them in more of the olive oil.

Arrange the platter by rolling each of the lengths of eggplant, zucchini, and carrots, then fanning them on the plate. Intersperse the rolled vegetables with the mushrooms, sun-dried tomatoes, peppers, and the mixed olives.

Drizzle the entire platter with remaining olive oil and reduced balsamic vinegar to taste and serve. This dish can easily be done a day or two ahead; just be sure to bring up to room temperature before serving and wait until serving to finish it with the final drizzling of olive oil and vinegar.

ARANCINE (Rice Balls)

MAKES 12 LARGE RICE BALLS

From:

Mike's Deli and Arthur Avenue Caterers

david and his father, michele "pops" greco

Ingredients:

4 cups Italian (arborio) white rice
1 packet saffron (.5 grams or .04 ounces)
1 tablespoon salt
$^1/_2$ tablespoon pepper
$^1/_4$ pound grated pecorino cheese ($^1/_2$ cup)
1$^1/_4$ pounds grated dry white mozzarella
10 large eggs
Oil for deep frying
1 tablespoon olive oil
$^1/_2$ medium onion, diced
1 garlic clove, diced
$^1/_2$ pound chopped meat
$^1/_2$ cup tomato sauce
$^1/_4$ cup green peas
1 pound bread crumbs

Directions:

Cook the rice in 8 cups of water with the saffron and salt to taste to al dente, about 15 to 20 minutes. Spoon rice into a large bowl or spread onto a sheet pan to cool. When the rice has cooled, mix in the salt, pepper, grated pecorino, and $^1/_2$ pound of the mozzarella; stir in 2 whisked eggs.

Heat the oil for deep frying, about 360° F.

To make the center stuffing, heat the olive oil in a sauté pan over medium-high heat and sauté the onion for 3 minutes; add the garlic and brown the onion, stirring, about 7 minutes. Add the chopped meat and sauté until cooked all the way through, about 8 minutes. Stir in the tomato sauce and peas, bring to a simmer, and cook until the peas are just cooked through, about 3 or 4 minutes. Let the mixture cool completely, then stir in the remaining mozzarella.

Fill a wide shallow bowl with water and dip the palms of your hands in it before rolling rice balls. Roll the rice mixture into large balls, about 3 inches in diameter. While holding the ball of rice in the palm of your hand, gently push the thumb of your other hand three quarters of the way into the rice ball, making a rather large round indentation, then stuff the ball with a couple tablespoons of the chopped meat mixture. Seal the meat inside the ball with more rice and, using your palms, roll the ball gently to reshape. Continue with the rest of the rice and meat mixture until done. Whisk the remaining 8 eggs in a bowl, coat the rice balls in the egg, then in the bread crumbs, and coat completely—repeat this three times. Fry until deep golden, about 4 to 6 minutes, and set on paper towels to drain. Serve warm or at room temperature.

Stuffed rice balls, called *arancine,* are common street food in Sicily. The name refers to their orangelike appearance.

BOCCONCINI SALAD

MAKES 4 SERVINGS

From:

Casa Della Mozzarella

adapted from a recipe by Orazio Carciotto

Ingredients:

2 cups cherry tomatoes
1 pound bocconcini (small mozzarella balls)
1 tablespoon chopped fresh oregano or basil,
plus whole leaves for garnish
2 garlic cloves, minced
$1/4$ cup olive oil
Salt and pepper to taste

Tip:

You can substitute slices of mozzarella in this recipe if you can't find bocconcini, just make sure it's freshly made.

Directions:

Slice each of the cherry tomatoes in half and toss in a bowl with the bocconcini, chopped herb, garlic, oil, and salt and pepper. Serve on a platter garnished with herb leaves.

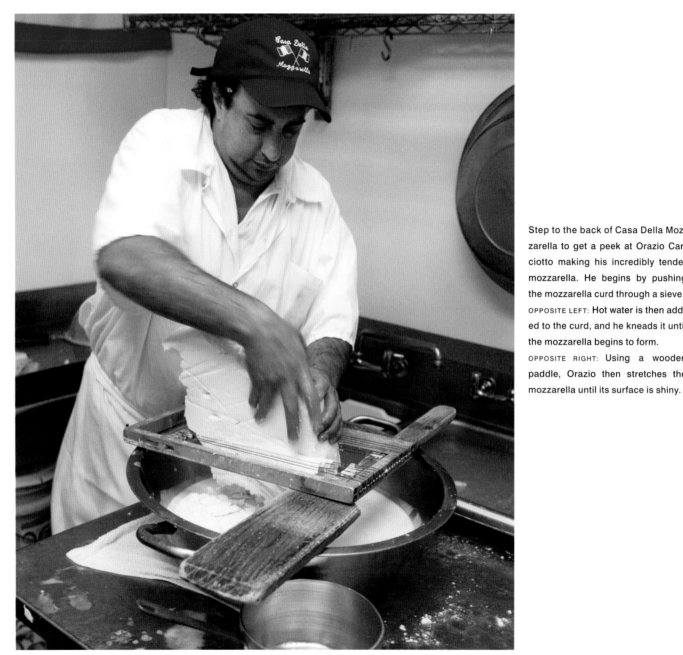

Step to the back of Casa Della Mozzarella to get a peek at Orazio Carciotto making his incredibly tender mozzarella. He begins by pushing the mozzarella curd through a sieve.

OPPOSITE LEFT: Hot water is then added to the curd, and he kneads it until the mozzarella begins to form.

OPPOSITE RIGHT: Using a wooden paddle, Orazio then stretches the mozzarella until its surface is shiny.

Once the mozzarella is ready to work, he stretches and folds it into balls or ties it into knots to make bocconcini, after which they are placed in salted or unsalted water until purchased.

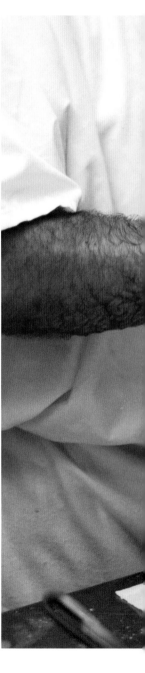

FRIED SMOKED MOZZARELLA

MAKES 6 TO 8 SERVINGS

From:

Casa Della Mozzarella

adapted from a recipe by Orazio Carciotto

Ingredients:

1/4 cup olive oil for frying
1 pound fresh smoked mozzarella,
   sliced into 1/2-inch rounds
1 cup flour
1 egg, beaten with 2 tablespoons milk
2 cups bread crumbs
Salt to taste

Directions:

Over medium-high heat, heat the olive oil in a medium skillet. Flour each slice of mozzarella, dip the slices in the egg mixture, and coat with bread crumbs. Fry the mozzarella slices in single-layer batches, turning when browned on bottom side, about 2 minutes. Remove with a slotted spoon or spatula, and drain on paper towels. Salt to taste and serve.

Tip:

This tantalizing appetizer shines when served on a bed of arugula that has been lightly tossed with lemon vinaigrette.

ZUCCHINI FRITTI

MAKES 6 SERVINGS

From:

Mario's Restaurant

Joseph Migliucci

Ingredients:

3 zucchini, about ¹/₂ pound each
Flour for dredging
3 eggs, beaten
Oil for deep frying
Salt to taste

Crispy additions to a spread of antipasti, these zucchini also complement simply prepared fish recipes (Red Snapper with Lemon, page 118).

Directions:

Trim the ends off the zucchini. Cut them into 3-inch lengths, and cut each piece lengthwise into flat ¹/₄-inch-thick slices (you want them to be rectangular; do not cut them into rounds). Then cut the slices into ¹/₄-inch strips (they should look like 3-inch matchsticks). Drop the strips into cold water and let stand 1 minute.

Drain and pat the zucchini dry on paper towels. In a bowl, sprinkle the zucchini with just enough flour to thinly coat, tossing gently with your hands.

In a large bowl, place the beaten eggs. Add the floured zucchini and combine them with the eggs, tossing with your hands until the zucchini is coated.

Heat about 1 to 2 inches of oil to about 375° F. Fry the zucchini in batches, stirring to separate the pieces, about 1 to 2 minutes each, or until crisp. Set aside on a paper towel to drain. Sprinkle with salt and serve immediately.

SAUTÉED ESCAROLE

MAKES 4 SERVINGS

From:

Mike's Deli and Arthur Avenue Caterers

david and his father, michele "pops" greco

Ingredients:

1 head escarole
2 to 3 tablespoons extra-virgin olive oil
4 to 5 garlic cloves
Salt and pepper to taste

Directions:

Heat a medium pot of water over high heat for blanching and prepare a large bowl of ice water for shocking.

Trim and clean the escarole. Blanch it in the boiling water for about 1 minute. Remove and shock for 1 minute in ice water to set the color. Remove and drain. In a medium sauté pan over medium heat, heat 1 tablespoon olive oil. Sauté the garlic cloves until deep brown on all sides, being careful not to burn them, about 4 to 5 minutes. Chop the escarole and add to the pan. Stir for 1 minute and season with salt and pepper. Serve drizzled with additional olive oil.

If you're not familiar with escarole, it belongs to the chicory family, along with Belgian endive and curly endive, and can serve as an all-purpose side dish. David also likes to use it in some of his famous sandwiches.

SPIEDINI ALLA ROMANA

MAKES 8 TO 12 SERVINGS

From:

Mario's Restaurant

Joseph Migliucci

Sandwich Ingredients:

14 slices white bread (supermarket-style)
1 large round of mozzarella cheese,
  sliced about ¼ inch thick or slightly thicker
Flour for dredging
5 eggs, well beaten
Oil for deep frying

Anchovy Sauce:

8 tablespoons butter
10 anchovies
1 tablespoon finely chopped parsley
¼ cup drained capers (optional)
½ cup brown beef gravy (canned)

Directions:

Trim the crusts from the bread slices and slice them in half to create 28 rectangles. Cut 14 pieces of mozzarella to fit the size and shape of the rectangles as closely as possible. Make 14 mozzarella sandwiches. Skewer the sandwiches with 2 skewers each to hold the sandwiches together while they cook.

Dredge all the skewered sandwiches in flour. Dip them thoroughly in the egg and place the sandwiches on a rack. This may be done a half hour or so in advance.

Preheat the oven to 400° F.

Heat the oil over medium-high heat for deep frying. When the oil is very hot, almost smoking, add the sandwiches. Cook about 3 minutes, turning once, or until golden brown all over. It may be necessary to fry the sandwiches in two batches. Drain on paper towels.

In a saucepan over medium-high heat, combine the sauce ingredients and simmer, stirring, for 3 to 4 minutes, or until the anchovies are "melted" and the sauce is smooth.

Place the skewered sandwiches on a buttered ovenproof dish and bake about 5 minutes or until piping hot throughout. Remove the skewers and cut each sandwich crosswise into two or three portions. Serve with the anchovy sauce spooned on top.

These are skewered, deep-fried mozzarella sandwiches served with a zesty anchovy sauce.

MELANZANE RIPIENI WITH MARINARA SAUCE

MAKE 8 TO 12 SERVINGS

From:

Mario's Restaurant

Joseph Migliucci

Eggplant Ingredients:

Oil for deep frying
1 ¹/₂ pounds eggplant
  Flour for dredging
3 large eggs
2 tablespoons finely chopped parsley

Filling Ingredients:

¹/₂ pound mozzarella cheese,
  cut into quarter-inch cubes
¹/₂ cup finely shredded ham, preferably prosciutto
1 egg
2 cups ricotta cheese
¹/₄ cup grated Parmesan cheese
1 tablespoon finely chopped parsley
Salt and ground pepper to taste
2 to 3 cups Marinara Sauce (page 48)

Tip:

When choosing the eggplants for this recipe, make sure to buy them large enough to accommodate the length of the strips (8 inches).

Directions:

Preheat the oven to 500° F. Heat the oil for deep frying over medium-high heat.

Trim off the ends of the eggplant and cut lengthwise into 8-inch long slices. This should be about 12 center-cut slices. Discard the trimmings. Dredge the slices in flour to coat all sides. Shake off the excess. In a bowl, beat the 3 eggs with 2 tablespoons parsley. Dip the eggplant slices in the egg to coat well. Fry the slices, a few at a time in hot oil, about 3 minutes for each batch, or until browned. Drain well.

To make the filling, in a medium bowl, combine the mozzarella with the ham, egg, ricotta, Parmesan, parsley, and salt and pepper.

Place the fried eggplant slices on a flat surface. Add equal amounts of filling toward the base of each slice. Roll to enclose the filling.

Spoon about half an inch of Marinara Sauce into a baking dish large enough to hold the stuffed slices. Arrange them on top of the sauce. Cover with more sauce and place in the oven. Bake about 10 minutes, or until bubbling, and the cheese has melted, then serve.

Teitel Brothers

Profile

2372 Arthur Avenue
Bronx, NY 10458
718-733-9400
http://www.teitelbros.com

Now in its third generation, Teitel Brothers has been serving the Arthur Avenue community since 1915. The maze of anchovy cans, wheels of imported cheese, barrels of dried legumes and olives, lines of dried sausage that fill this corner store are top quality and well-priced. While they have an extensive mail-order business these days, the old-time grocery atmosphere is not to be missed. When you visit, note the Star of David formed in the entryway tiles; the Teitel family immigrated from Austria and was one of the few Jewish merchants in the neighborhood.

TRICOLOR PEPPERS WITH REDUCED BALSAMIC

MAKES 4 SERVINGS

From:

Mike's Deli and Arthur Avenue Caterers

david and his father, michele "pops" greco

Ingredients:

1 red bell pepper
1 yellow bell pepper
1 orange bell pepper
2 to 3 tablespoons extra-virgin olive oil
1 tablespoon chopped fresh oregano
Salt and pepper to taste
Reduced balsamic vinegar, for drizzling

Directions:

Preheat the broiler or a grill to high.

Cut the peppers in half and seed and devein them. Brush them with some of the olive oil. Roast them over the grill or under the broiler for about 2 to 3 minutes or until just beginning to color, turning once. Do not overcook them; they should be al dente, with a hint of crispness. Slice them into 1-inch-thick strips and toss them with about 1 tablespoon of the remaining olive oil, the oregano, and salt and pepper. Serve on a platter and drizzle with reduced balsamic vinegar.

Tip:

David also suggests adding sautéed onions to this dish, but doesn't here because "Papa Greco doesn't like onions."

SAUTÉED BROCCOLI RABE

MAKES 4 SERVINGS

From:

Mike's Deli and Arthur Avenue Café

david and his father, michele "pops" greco

Ingredients:

1 pound broccoli rabe, tough stems trimmed away
2 to 3 tablespoons extra-virgin olive oil
4 to 5 garlic cloves
Salt and pepper to taste

Directions:

Heat a large pot of water over high heat and prepare a large bowl of ice water for shocking.

Cut the broccoli rabe into 3-inch lengths. Blanch it in the boiling water for about 1 minute. Remove and shock it for 1 minute in ice water to set the color. Remove and drain. In a medium sauté pan over medium heat, heat 1 tablespoon olive oil. Sauté the garlic cloves until deep brown on all sides, being careful not to burn them, about 4 to 5 minutes. Add the broccoli rabe to the pan. Sauté for about 3 minutes. Season with salt and pepper and serve drizzled with additional olive oil.

This slightly bitter green is very popular in Italy as a versatile side dish. It's also delicious sautéed with slices of fresh sausage.

RECIPES

Pasta

Profiles:

Borgatti's Ravioli & Egg Noodles

Mario's Restaurant

MARIO BORGATTI borgatti's ravioli & egg noodles

Profile

632 East 187th Street
Bronx, NY 10458
718-367-3799

Located directly across the street from Our Lady of Mount Carmel Church, Borgatti's has been selling fresh egg noodles and ravioli since it opened in 1935. Point to the width you want on the cardboard sheet and they'll cut it to order, toss it with cornmeal, and bundle it in paper. They've always made just two kinds of ravioli: spinach and meat, and ricotta. (None of this chocolate ravioli business!) These are their staples, but that's not to say they haven't kept up with the times; they also sell mushroom, no-yolk, spinach, whole wheat, tomato, and carrot noodles.

MARIO'S PARENTS, Lindo and Maria Borgatti, came from the region of Emilia-Romagna, near Bologna, but met in Boston and were married in 1907. An importing job brought them to New York that same year, where they lived on Morton Street. Several years later Lindo and a few partners opened a grocery store on Arthur Avenue and 188th Street, and the Borgattis settled in Belmont.

Standing behind the counter of his bustling shop on a sunny Saturday afternoon, Mario shares some early memories:

"In 1935 we were in the midst of a very big depression. And as I remember I was just graduating high school that year and I used to see signs in the bus going to school that said there were 15 million unemployed in this country—that was over 30 percent. [My father] found himself without work and they decided to open up this type of shop in a store about a block and a half away from here. They opened up in November 1935. Then some months later there was an opportunity for him to move here with the shop. It was like half of this shop. None of this stuff was here." Mario gestures toward the equipment. "They started out hand-rolling pasta and, for a while, hand-cutting until they picked up this machine—which was already old in 1935—to make three different cuts of noodles, and a small machine like this here that mixes and rolls out the pasta and has an attached cutter. It was the first part of 1936, and business progressed. In WWII, the armed forces took in about 15 million young men . . . the unemployment figure!" Mario laughs. "That's when the ladies became riveters and so on. Well, people were closer together; there were so many young men conscripted from this neighborhood. They used to have flags flying across the street with big banners with stars on and when they would get word of a GI dying they would put another star on. The churches became very crowded. That's how it is during a war like that."

Mario started in the business upon its opening, working there until he went into the Navy for 3 1/2 years. He was discharged in 1946, but in the meantime, he was married in 1943 and had his first child in 1944. They ended up with three boys and two girls.

Mario was one of six sons, and they all helped out the family, holding a variety of jobs. One brother worked for the Agricultural Administration under Franklin D. Roosevelt. Two other brothers worked for the Interboro Rapid Transit Service, the grandparent of our subway system, and another worked for a firm that made and sold yarns to dress shops.

After Mario's discharge in 1946, the Borgattis invested in a new type of machinery to make the ravioli, because they used to make them by hand, and they also expanded their business into the space next door. Asked whether there were other pasta makers in the neighborhood at the time Mario replies, "There were three others but you see, they used to make the pasta in packages, that type. We made only egg noodles and ravioli. See, where my parents came from egg noodles were part of the staple

there. That was an everyday affair at home. They went in on a shoestring; you know they had children at home."

The family tradition continues, with Mario's son Chris running the store alongside him, and Mario is confident in the future of the business. "I don't know why but since we opened in the depression we've never really felt the effects of any depression. If you stay here a while you can see people coming in. We more or less have made a mark. Even that little young lady wants to buy something"—he smiles at a little girl "that's pretty cute."

Surrounded by his original equipment, rolling out and cutting the sheets of pasta, Mario takes neighborhood changes in stride. "When people tell me the neighborhood has changed I tell them when my parents came to the neighborhood [in 1917]. I was born in this neighborhood 85 plus years ago. At that time the neighborhood was Irish and German and I'm sure they were saying, 'The neighborhood is changing.' Right? So it became 95 percent Italian, you know. You should see the holidays, it's sort of an oasis . . . Our customers are unique; they wait on line on the holidays. I don't know how they do it; I don't think I would." He chuckles. "They have such patience, they're good-natured . . . I haven't had to change the recipe. We use the best quality that we can get, and the world beats a pathway to our door. And we keep to a quality product, not wholesale, just retail, at least not yet.

You know the secret?
You make them the way your grandmother did."

THE ARTHUR AVENUE COOKBOOK ANN VOLKWEIN

MANICOTTI

MAKES 4 SERVINGS

"We made only egg noodles and ravioli.

See, where my parents came from egg noodles were part of the staple there.

That was an everyday affair at home..."

From:

Borgatti's Ravioli & Egg Noodles

Mario and Chris Borgatti

Ingredients:

1 pound ricotta
1 whole egg
1/4 cup grated Parmesan cheese
2 tablespoons minced parsley
Salt and pepper to taste
8 squares of fresh manicotti noodles
Marinara Sauce (page 48)

The simple ingredients and flavors of this dish make it palatable for the youngest Borgatti customers. You can buy prestuffed manicotti at the shop.

Directions:

Preheat the oven to 375° F and set a large pot of water on the stove top to boil.

In a bowl, combine the ricotta, egg, Parmesan, parsley, and salt and pepper. Set this filling aside.

Cook the manicotti in boiling water for 1 minute. After they've cooked for 1 minute, remove the pot from the heat but do not drain the manicotti squares in a colander as the noodles often stick together. Instead, run cold water into the pot until you can fish the manicotti squares out safely with your fingers. Shake off the excess water as you remove each square. It is usually best to place the squares on a clean cloth to further blot them.

Lay the squares flat on a cloth, placing the filling across the center of the dough, leaving a little room at the edges on each side. Turn up the edge nearest you so that it lies on top of the filling. Now turn the edge farthest from you toward you so that it lies on top of the first edge. You now have a cannoli-like tube. Spread one ladleful of the sauce onto the bottom of a 9 x 12-inch baking pan. Turn the manicotti over and place seam side down in the baking pan on top of the sauce. Continue until the pan has a layer of manicotti. Spoon two more ladlefuls of sauce over the top and bake for 45 minutes. Remove from the oven and let sit 10 minutes before serving. Serve with additional sauce for individual servings.

MARINARA SAUCE

MAKES ABOUT 5 CUPS

From:

Borgatti's Ravioli & Egg Noodles

Mario and Chris Borgatti

Ingredients:

¹/₃ **cup olive oil**

2 garlic cloves, thinly sliced

Salt and freshly ground pepper to taste

Two 28-ounce cans peeled,
  crushed plum tomatoes with liquid

10 basil leaves, chopped, or 1 tablespoon dried

1 tablespoon chopped parsley, or 1 teaspoon dried

Everyone has his own variation of Marinara Sauce. Borgatti's is basic and can be used throughout this book whenever marinara is called for—the seasonings and herbs can be adjusted to taste.

Directions:

In a medium saucepan over medium-low heat, heat the oil. Sauté the garlic, salt, and pepper for 5 minutes or until the garlic is softened. Add the remaining ingredients, then raise the heat to medium-high, and bring to a simmer, stirring often. Simmer for 30 minutes. The sauce can be stored for up to 5 days in the refrigerator and several months in the freezer.

FETTUCCINE ALFREDO

MAKES 4 SERVINGS

Ingredients:

1 pound fettuccine

6 ounces butter

¹/₂ **cup heavy cream**

¹/₂ **cup grated Parmesan cheese**

1 egg yolk

Freshly ground black pepper to taste

Tip:

Plan to whisk up this Roman sauce just before serving for best results.

Directions:

Prepare a double boiler and bring 6 to 8 quarts of salted water to a boil. While the fettuccine boils (note that Borgatti's fresh fettuccine cooks in just 4 to 5 minutes; store-bought dried pasta may take 11 to 12 minutes), carefully melt the butter in the top of the double boiler. Add the heavy cream and half of the Parmesan cheese, whisking constantly. Drain the noodles and quickly toss them in a bowl with the hot sauce and the egg yolk. Mix rapidly so as to serve piping hot. Add the rest of the grated cheese and freshly ground pepper to individual portions, as desired.

BOLOGNESE-STYLE MEAT SAUCE

MAKES 4 SERVINGS OVER PASTA

From:

Borgatti's Ravioli & Egg Noodles

Mario and Chris Borgatti

Ingredients:

$^1/_3$ cup olive oil

2 ounces diced salt pork

1 garlic clove, finely chopped

$^1/_2$ cup chopped onion

1 cup chopped carrot

1 cup chopped celery

1 pound ground lean beef

$^1/_2$ cup white wine

$^1/_2$ cup light cream

1 tablespoon tomato paste

2 cups beef broth (or one 28-ounce can peeled, crushed tomatoes may be substituted)

1 cup peas

2 ounces butter

Salt and pepper to taste

$^1/_2$ teaspoon ground nutmeg

Bolognese is the granddaddy of all Italian-American meat sauces; Borgatti's does it justice, deeply rich and flavorful.

Directions:

In a medium saucepan over medium-high heat, heat the oil and sauté the diced salt pork until the pork is light brown, about 5 minutes. Remove the salt pork with a slotted spoon and set aside. Add the garlic to the oil and sauté until golden brown, about 3 minutes. Add the onion and cook until translucent, about 5 to 7 minutes. Add the carrot and celery and cook until they soften and begin to change color, about 6 to 7 minutes. Add the ground beef and cook until browned, about 8 to 10 minutes. Pour in the wine, raise the heat to high, and bring to a simmer while stirring. Pour in the cream and bring to a boil for 3 minutes. In a medium bowl, dilute the tomato paste in the beef broth and add to the saucepan. Add the peas to the saucepan, cover and allow to simmer for 45 minutes. Add the butter, salt, pepper, and nutmeg. Stir well and simmer for 15 minutes more. Serve over spaghetti or another long pasta.

FETTUCCINE ALLA CARBONARA

MAKES 4 SERVINGS

From:

Borgatti's Ravioli & Egg Noodles

Mario and Chris Borgatti

Ingredients:

1 pound fettuccine
8 strips bacon
6 ounces thickly sliced prosciutto
6 ounces unsalted butter
2 tablespoons minced onion
$^1/_3$ cup white wine
$^1/_2$ cup heavy cream
$^1/_2$ cup milk
1 tablespoon minced parsley
$^1/_2$ cup grated Parmesan cheese
1 egg yolk
Freshly ground black pepper to taste

Tip:

The toothsome quality of al dente fettuccine is married here to a completely decadent sauce. Try serving this dish as a brunch alternative—a creative way to satisfy a bacon-and-eggs craving.

Directions:

Set a large pot of salted water to boil for the pasta.

In a large sauté pan over medium-high heat, fry the bacon until crisp. Drain the bacon slices thoroughly. Cut the prosciutto and bacon into $^1/_2$-inch squares. In a medium saucepan over low heat, melt the butter. Add the minced onion and sauté over low heat until translucent, about 5 minutes. Add the bacon and the prosciutto to the saucepan. Stir over low heat for 3 to 4 minutes. Pour the wine into the saucepan and raise the heat to medium. Stirring, bring the mixture to a low boil and cook for 5 minutes. Add the cream and milk and then bring to a low boil again, cook for 5 minutes. Meanwhile, boil the pasta to al dente (just cooked through), then drain. Reduce the heat under the saucepan to low, add the parsley and approximately half of the grated cheese. Pour this mixture over the pasta. Add the egg yolk and toss the pasta and sauce together thoroughly. Add the remaining grated cheese and freshly ground pepper to individual portions. Serve immediately.

LASAGNE

MAKES 6 TO 8 SERVINGS

From:

Borgatti's Ravioli & Egg Noodles

Mario and Chris Borgatti

Ingredients:

1 1/2 pounds fresh lasagne noodles
1 pound ricotta
1 whole egg
1/4 cup grated Parmesan cheese
2 tablespoons minced parsley
Salt and pepper to taste
1 pound sweet, precooked Italian sausage, crumbled
1 pound mozzarella, cut into thin slices
   (easier to slice while chilled)
Marinara Sauce (page 48)

Tip:

Dried lasagna noodles will work if you can't find fresh ones; just be sure to parboil them to al dente (just cooked through, still firm).

Directions:

Preheat the oven to 375° F. Set a large pot of water to boil for the pasta.

In a bowl, combine the ricotta, egg, Parmesan, parsley, and salt and pepper. Set this filling aside.

Cook the lasagne strips in boiling water for 1 minute. Remove from the heat but do not drain in a colander as the noodles often stick together. Instead, run cold water into the pot until you can carefully fish the lasagne strips out with your fingers. Shake off the excess water as you remove each square. It is usually best to place the strips on a clean cloth to further blot them.

Spread a ladleful of sauce onto the bottom of a 9 x 13-inch baking pan. Cover the bottom of the pan with a layer of lasagne strips. Spread a layer of the ricotta filling on top of the lasagne, then a layer of sauce, a layer of sausage, and a layer of mozzarella. Place a layer of lasagne strips on top of the mozzarella then repeat layering the ricotta mixture, sauce, sausage, and mozzarella. Repeat this layering process until you have filled the pan, ending with a layer of pasta covered with sauce and topped off with mozzarella.

Bake for 45 minutes. Remove from the oven and let sit for 10 minutes, then serve accompanied by additional sauce for individual servings.

RECIPE

MARIO'S RESTAURANT

joseph migliucci

Profile

2342 Arthur Avenue
Bronx, NY 10458
718-584-1188

You may have seen the episode of *The Sopranos* shot here, or maybe you're familiar with the restaurant's mention in *The Godfather* (the original novel, not the film, the family didn't want that sort of publicity).

MARIO'S is a true Arthur Avenue institution, with a celebrity-dotted history, from Governor Rockefeller to Liz Taylor. Chef/owner Joseph Migliucci carries on the tradition that his father, Mario, began in 1919. Originally a pizzeria, Mario's still serves superlative thin-crust pies, which you should ask for politely—but you won't find them on the menu. There you'll discover a broad range of no-nonsense Neapolitan dishes cooked with the Italian-American flair that defines the Avenue.

ABOVE: Outside Mario's Restaurant. RIGHT: A portrait of the founder of Mario's Restaurant, enshrined in a rotating clock at the back of the dining room. OPPOSITE: Joseph Migliucci

P
A
S
T
A

GNOCCHI DI PATATE WITH FILETTI DI POMODORO

MAKES 6 (OR MORE) SERVINGS

From:

Mario's Restaurant

Joseph Migliucci

Ingredients:

**3 large potatoes, preferably Idaho,
about 1 3/4 pounds total, peeled
Salt to taste
2 egg yolks
1 3/4 to 2 cups flour
6 tablespoons melted butter (optional)
Grated Parmesan cheese (optional)
2 cups Filetti de Pomodoro (page 55)
Freshly ground black pepper to taste**

Directions:

Place the potatoes in a large pot and add cold water to cover. Add salt to taste and bring to a boil over high heat. After it reaches a boil, reduce the heat and simmer until the potatoes are tender, but not mushy. Drain and let cool.

Peel the potatoes. Put them through a ricer or food mill. In a bowl, add the egg yolks to the potatoes and blend well.

Scoop the potatoes onto a flat surface and start kneading them, adding the flour gradually. Add only enough flour to make a firm, but still soft and delicate dough. If too much flour is added the gnocchi become tough when cooked. Knead thoroughly, then shape the dough, rolling with your palms to make a thick sausage shape, about 11 or 12 inches long. Using a knife or pastry scraper, cut the roll into eleven equal slices. Roll each slice into a long cigar shape. Cut each cigar into 18 or 19 pieces. These pieces will resemble miniature pillows. Flour the pieces and set aside until ready to cook.

In a large pot, bring a large quantity of salted water to a boil. Drop half the pieces of dough into the water then bring the heat down to medium. Let cook until they rise to the surface, about 5 minutes. Drain quickly and chill in a bowl of cold water for about 30 seconds. Drain well. Repeat with remaining gnocchi.

When ready to serve, drop the pieces once more into a large quantity of boiling salted water. When they float, drain them, then return them to the empty pot. Add the melted butter and cheese, if desired. Add the Filetti di Pomodoro sauce and sprinkle with pepper. Serve with additional sauce on the side.

Gnocchi making takes some getting used to but the results are worthwhile—tender little pillows that are utterly unlike the store-bought varieties.

FILETTI DI POMODORO
(TOMATO AND ONION SAUCE)

MAKES ABOUT 6 CUPS

From:

Mario's Restaurant

Joseph Migliucci

Directions:

In a medium bowl, crush the tomatoes with your hands. In a medium saucepan over medium to medium-low heat, melt the lard and sauté the onions, stirring often, until the onions are golden brown, about 20 minutes (you want them to caramelize). Raise the heat to medium-high, add the ham, and sauté about 5 minutes. Add the tomatoes and simmer about 2 hours, stirring often to prevent sticking. Add the salt, pepper, and basil.

Ingredients:

Two 32-ounce cans plum tomatoes with liquid, preferably imported from Italy
$1/4$ pound lard
3 cups thinly sliced onions
$1/3$ pound ham, preferably prosciutto, cut into very thin strips, about $1^{1}/_{2}$ cups
Salt and freshly ground pepper to taste
$1/4$ cup freshly snipped basil leaves, or 1 tablespoon dried crushed

Tip:

The sauce can be refrigerated for 5 days or frozen for several months.

SALSA MONACHINA

MAKES ABOUT 4 1/2 CUPS

From:

Mario's Restaurant

Joseph Migliucci

Ingredients:

**Two 28-ounce cans plum tomatoes,
    preferably imported from Italy**
$^2/_3$ cup olive oil
1 tablespoon thinly sliced garlic
**1$^1/_4$ cups capers, preferably salt-cured
    rather than packed in vinegar**
15 pitted black California olives, sliced
5 whole anchovies
Salt and freshly ground pepper to taste

Directions:

In a large bowl, crush the tomatoes with your hands. In a large saucepan, heat the oil over medium-high heat. Add the garlic. Cook until lightly browned, about 4 to 5 minutes. Rinse the salt off the capers and add them to the pan. Add the olives and anchovies and cook until the anchovies "melt," about 5 minutes.

Add the tomatoes and reduce the heat to simmer. Cook, stirring occasionally, about 1 1/2 hours. Add salt and pepper to taste. The sauce can be kept in the refrigerator up to 5 days, or frozen for several months.

Tip:

Salsa Monachina is akin to a puttanesca sauce—packed with the piquant flavors of the Mediterranean. Serve tossed with spaghetti or linguine.

SICILIAN BAKED
ZITI CATANIA-STYLE
MAKES 16 SERVINGS

From:

Orazio and Philomena Carciotto

Ingredients :

$^1/_2$ cup olive oil
1 medium onion, chopped
1 $^1/_2$ pounds ground beef
Two 35-ounce cans pureed tomato
Salt and pepper to taste
2 tablespoons sugar
6 hard-boiled eggs
1 pound dry mozzarella
1 medium eggplant
2 pounds ziti
$^1/_2$ pound grated Parmigiano-Reggiano
  (or other Parmesan cheese)
2 beaten eggs
Butter for greasing pans

Orazio and his wife like to do all the prep work for this
family-style meal on a Sunday—then all they have to do is
boil the pasta and stick it in the oven during the week.

Directions:

To make the sauce, heat 2 tablespoons of the olive oil in a medium
saucepan over medium-high heat. Sauté the onion until soft and
translucent, about 5 minutes. Add the beef and brown it, stirring
often, about 10 to 15 minutes. Add the tomato puree and salt and
pepper to taste. Let cook at least 1 $^1/_2$ hours uncovered over very
low heat. Stir in the sugar after 1 hour has passed and skim the fat.
Set aside.

Preheat the oven to 400° F and set a large pot of water to boil on
the stove top for pasta. Grease two large (9 x 13 x 2-inch) baking pans
with butter on all sides.

Slice the eggs into about 4 to 5 slices each. Slice the mozzarella.
With a vegetable peeler, skin the eggplant, then cut it into 1/4-inch-
thick slices. Brush the eggplant slices lightly with oil and place in a
large skillet set over medium-high heat. Fry the eggplant slices, in
batches, until cooked through and soft. Boil the ziti in salted water
until al dente, not completely cooked through, and drain, about 8
minutes. Depending on the size of your pot, you may have to boil the
pasta in two batches.

Mix 2 tablespoons Parmesan cheese and some salt and pepper
with the beaten eggs. Toss the ziti with a ladleful of the sauce. Place
half the pasta in the bottom of the prepared pans. Layer the boiled
egg slices on top. Layer the mozzarella on top of the eggs. Layer the
eggplant slices on top of the mozzarella. Place the remaining ziti on
top of the eggplant. Pour the reserved sauce over the ziti. Sprinkle
the grated Parmesan cheese on top of the sauce. Drizzle the beaten
egg and Parmesan mixture over the cheese. Bake for 30 to 45 minutes, checking often. When a fork comes out clean, the dish is ready.
The top should be a little burned. Orazio says, "Don't worry about
the burnt bits, it's supposed to be that way." Let cool at least 15 minutes before serving or slicing. (It's even better the next day!)

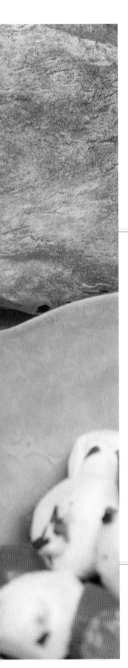

PENNE AMATRICIANA
MAKES 4 SERVINGS

From:

Biancardi Meats
Sal Biancardi

Ingredients :

Salt to taste
4 tablespoons olive oil
$^1/_3$ pound pancetta, diced
$^1/_2$ cup thinly sliced onion
3 garlic cloves, minced
$^1/_3$ cup dry white wine
1 32-ounce can Italian plum tomatoes
1 teaspoon ground black pepper
1 pound penne
$^1/_4$ cup grated Parmigiano-Reggiano

The typical Roman Amatriciana sauce adds a dash of spicy red pepper. Sal's version includes a healthy dose of black pepper instead, but does use the classic, unsmoked Italian bacon, pancetta.

Directions:

Bring salted water to a boil for the pasta.

In a large sauté pan, heat the olive oil over medium heat. Add the pancetta and cook until almost crisp, about 6 minutes. Add the onion and sauté until soft, about 4 to 5 more minutes, stirring often. Add the minced garlic and cook until light brown. Add the wine, deglaze the pan, and reduce the liquid by two-thirds. Add the tomatoes and, with a wooden spoon, break them up as they cook. Increase the heat to medium-high and bring the sauce to a rapid simmer. Simmer for 15 minutes. Meanwhile, cook the pasta until al dente. Season the sauce to taste with salt and pepper. Toss the pasta with the sauce. Serve with grated cheese on top.

CAPELLINI WITH CLAMS
MAKES 4 SERVINGS

From:

Randazzo Seafood
Adapted from a recipe by Frank Randazzo

Ingredients:

12 ounces capellini
2 tablespoons olive oil
4 garlic cloves, minced
1 1/2 pounds very small clams,
  such as New Zealand cockles, scrubbed
1/3 cup dry white wine
1 cup fish stock or clam juice
4 tablespoons chopped parsley
Salt and pepper to taste

Directions:

In a large pot, bring water to a boil for the pasta.

In a large skillet, heat the olive oil over medium-high heat, then add the garlic, and sauté until golden, about 2 to 3 minutes. Add the clams, white wine, and stock and cover. Allow to boil until the clams open, about 4 to 5 minutes. Meanwhile, boil the capellini in the water, which you've salted, until al dente. When all the clams have opened, discard the unopened ones. Stir the capellini and 3 tablespoons of the chopped parsley into the pan juices. Season with salt and pepper. Serve on a platter with the clams and sprinkle with the remaining parsley.

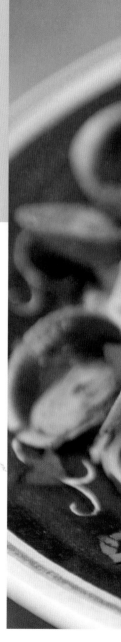

Tip:

Depending on personal taste, you can add hot chili flakes, lemon juice, or lemon zest to this recipe.

FARFALLE CON FUNGHI

MAKES 4 SERVINGS

From:

Mike's Deli and Arthur Avenue Caterers

david and his father, michele "pops" greco

Ingredients:

¹/₂ ounce dry porcini mushrooms
(2 ounces if you're feeling extravagant)
1 pound farfalle
2 tablespoons olive oil
3 shallots, peeled and diced
10 button mushrooms, sliced
4 ounces mascarpone
1 cup heavy cream
2 tablespoons grated Parmesan cheese
Salt and pepper to taste

Directions:

In a small saucepan, bring 1 pint of water to a boil, then add the porcini mushrooms. Allow to boil for 2 minutes. Turn the heat off and let mushrooms steep in hot water for 15 to 20 minutes. Meanwhile, bring a large pot of salted water to boil, add the pasta, and cook to al dente, about 7 to 8 minutes. In a medium sauté pan over medium-high heat, heat the oil then sauté the shallots until lightly browned, about 5 to 8 minutes. Drain the porcini mushrooms, saving the water. Chop them and add them along with the button mushrooms to the pan with the shallots. Sauté 4 to 5 minutes until the button mushrooms are lightly golden. Reduce the heat to medium and add the mascarpone and the cream. Stir slowly until everything blends. Add half the porcini mushroom water and the Parmesan cheese. Let this sauce reduce so it thickens a little, about 10 minutes. Stir in salt and pepper to taste. Remove from the heat and allow to come to room temperature. Put the mushroom mixture into the blender and mix until the mushrooms are in tiny pieces. Heat a large sauté pan over medium-high heat, add the mushroom sauce, and the farfalle. Mix well until heated through and serve hot.

David serves this pasta at the deli—bow ties with a cream sauce infused with the singular richness of the porcini mushroom. They may be expensive, but it's worth tracking down dried porcini. Dave sells them at the deli if you're in the area, or he'll send them to you if you call.

RIGATONI MELENZANA

MAKES 4 SERVINGS

From:

Mike's Deli and Arthur Avenue Caterers

david and his father, michele "pops" greco

Ingredients:

1 pound rigatoni
4 chicken breasts
1 tablespoon plus 1 teaspoon diced garlic
4 tablespoons olive oil
Salt and pepper to taste
1 small eggplant, diced into $1/4$-inch cubes
1 cup cream
2 tablespoons grated Parmesan cheese
$1^1/_2$ cups tomato sauce
20 spinach leaves, julienned

Directions:

Preheat the oven to 350° F. Heat the grill or a grill pan on the stove top over medium-high heat.

Bring a pot of lightly salted water to a boil, add the pasta, and cook to al dente, about 7 to 9 minutes. Drain the pasta. Clean the chicken and slice lengthwise into 1/2-inch-wide strips. In a mixing bowl, toss the chicken with 1 tablespoon of the garlic, 2 tablespoons of the olive oil, and salt and pepper. Grill the chicken for 2 to 3 minutes on each side, then place it on a sheet pan and bake it in the oven for 5 to 7 minutes. Remove the chicken from the oven, let cool, then cut it into smaller strips, about 1 inch long. In a large sauté pan over medium-high heat, heat the remaining olive oil and sauté the eggplant until cooked through, about 8 to 10 minutes. Add the cream, pasta, Parmesan, chicken, the remaining garlic, and mix well. Add the tomato sauce and spinach. Allow to heat through and serve.

Tips:

Rigatoni is served here with chicken in a pink eggplant sauce. The dish is rich with an almost meaty flavor and texture even without the chicken, which can easily be omitted for a vegetarian version.

RIGATONI ALLA ISABELLA

MAKES 4 SERVINGS

From:

Mike's Deli and Arthur Avenue Caterers

david and his father, michele "pops" greco

Ingredients :

1 pound rigatoni
4 chicken breasts
1 tablespoon diced garlic
4 tablespoons olive oil
Salt and pepper to taste
1 zucchini, trimmed and sliced thinly, lengthwise
2 cups heavy cream
4 tablespoons grated Parmesan cheese

David's Rigatoni alla Isabella is served with white cream sauce, grilled chicken, and grilled zucchini. The seasonings are delicate, letting the (too often overpowered) fresh, green flavor of the zucchini shine forth.

Directions:

Preheat the oven to 350° F. Heat the grill or a grill pan on the stove top over medium-high heat.

Bring a pot of lightly salted water to a boil, add the pasta, and cook to al dente, about 7 to 8 minutes. Drain the pasta. Slice the chicken breasts in half lengthwise. In a medium-size mixing bowl, combine the chicken, garlic, 2 tablespoons oil, and salt and pepper. Toss to coat the chicken well. Grill the chicken for 2 to 3 minutes on each side. Remove the chicken from the grill, place it on a sheet pan, and bake it in oven for 5 to 7 minutes. Meanwhile, toss the zucchini slices in 1 tablespoon of the oil, add salt and pepper, and place them on the grill, about 1 minute on each side, until well marked. Remove the chicken from the oven, allow it to cool, and cut it into 1-inch-long strips. Cut the zucchini crosswise into 1/2-inch pieces. In a large sauté pan over medium-high heat, add the remaining 1 tablespoon oil and the cream. Simmer until slightly thickened, about 8 minutes. Add the pasta, chicken, and zucchini, and stir until heated through. Add the Parmesan cheese, salt and pepper to taste, and serve.

RECIPES

Meat & Poultry

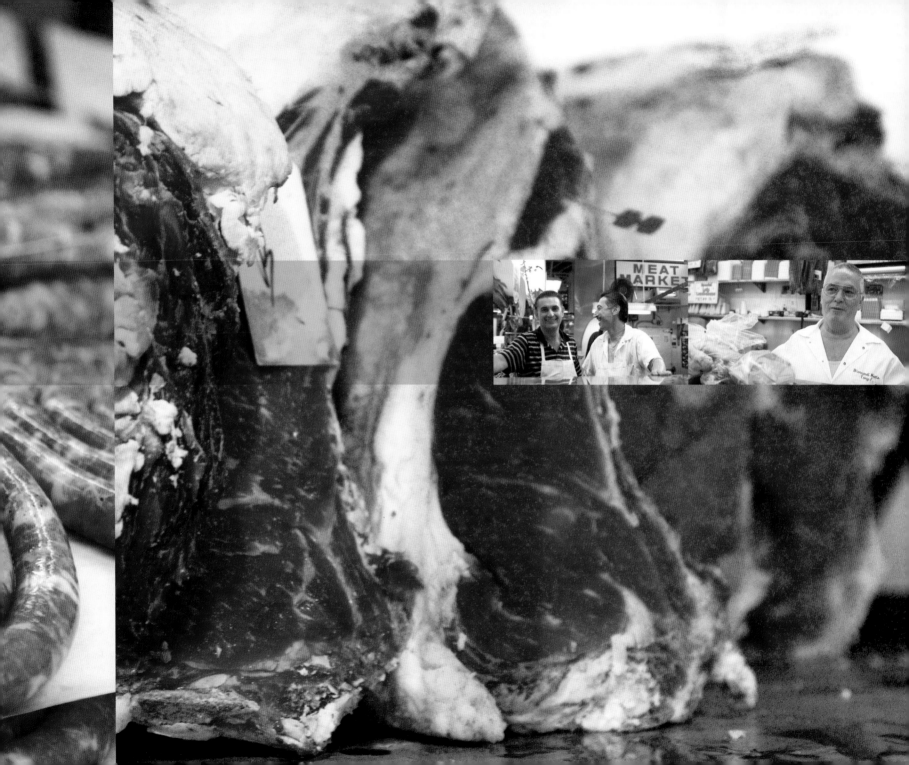

CALABRIA PORK STORE

Hundreds of sausages, in various states of aging, hang from the ceiling in this sliver of a shop, which sells authentic, hot and spicy Calabrese dried sausage. They have one with fennel seeds, an extra-hot version, and one with "a little bit of garlic." (I'd say! The garlic announces itself at the door.) Look for the Calabrese liver sausage and the flat sopressata, hot or sweet, pressed in the classic Italian manner.

Profile

2338 Arthur Avenue
Bronx, NY 10458
718-367-5145

MIKE'S DELI'S WORLD-FAMOUS PIZZA RUSTICA

MAKES 8 TO 10 SERVINGS

From:

Mike's Deli and Arthur Avenue Caterers

david and his father, michele "pops" greco

Pasta Frolla (Sweet Egg Pastry Crust) *Ingredients:*

4 cups flour, plus extra for rolling and kneading
4 eggs
1 1/2 sticks butter, cold, cut into small cubes
1 tablespoon grated lemon rind

Filling Ingredients:

1/2 large sopressata, about 4 ounces
1/2 large dry sausage, about 2 ounces
1/2 pound prosciutto
3/4 pound table cheese (such as pecorino)
3/4 pound basket cheese (or dry mozzarella)
1 1/2 pounds ricotta
6 eggs, plus 1 egg white
2/3 cup grated Romano cheese
1 tablespoon sugar
1 tablespoon chopped parsley

Tips:

A traditional Easter recipe that is served as a side dish during the Easter feast. Mike's sells loads of these to returning customers before the holiday. If you can't find basket cheese, call David and order it or substitute dry mozzarella.

Directions:

Preheat the oven to 350°F.

Scoop the flour onto the counter. Make a well in the middle and add the 4 eggs, butter, and lemon rind into the center. Gradually mix the ingredients into the flour with your hands. Knead until the dough is smooth. (Note: The dough can also be made in a food processor; to do so, gradually add the butter to the flour, processing until the butter is well distributed. Add the eggs and then the rind, processing until the dough comes together.) Refrigerate 1 hour before rolling out.

Cut the sopressata, dry sausage, prosciutto, table cheese, and basket cheese into small chunks (do not dice). In a bowl, mix the meat and table and basket cheeses with the ricotta. In a separate bowl, mix the 6 whole eggs, Romano, sugar, and parsley. When the mixture is smooth, stir in the meat and cheese mixture.

Roll the dough out and line a 10-inch springform pan with the dough, reserving one-third of the dough for the top crust. Set aside.

Pour the filling into the pan. Add the top crust, closing the edges well, pinching the dough. Make a few slits on top (you can punch airholes with a fork) and brush with the egg white. Bake for approximately 1 1/2 hours, checking after 30 minutes—punch more airholes if it looks like it may "blow up." Test with a toothpick—it should come out clean—or bake until the excess moisture evaporates from the top of the pie. Let cool and refrigerate overnight. You can slice the pie while still cool and heat the slices, but don't try to heat it before cutting it, or the slices will fall apart. Buona Pasqua a tutti!

BEEF SCALLOPINE CASALINGA

MAKES 8 SERVINGS

From:

Mario's Restaurant

Joseph Migliucci

Ingredients :

8 slices fillet of beef, each about $^1/_2$ inch thick
$^3/_4$ cup vegetable oil
$^1/_2$ cup finely chopped onion
$^1/_2$ cup very thin strips prosciutto
$^1/_3$ pound fresh mushrooms, thinly sliced
　(should be about 2 cups)
2 tablespoons butter
$^1/_3$ cup brown beef gravy (canned)
1 cup marsala wine
2 tablespoons finely chopped parsley
Flour for dredging
Oil for shallow frying
8 rounds mozzarella cheese, about $^1/_3$ inch thick
　and 3 inches in diameter

Beef fillets in a marsala mushroom sauce with mozzarella cheese melted on top—now that's old-style Italian-American cooking.

Directions:

Place the fillets on a flat surface and pound lightly with a flat mallet. Set aside.

In a skillet over medium-high temperature, heat the vegetable oil. Add the onion and cook, stirring often until lightly browned, about 10 minutes. Add the prosciutto and the mushrooms. Sauté slowly, about 10 minutes, stirring occasionally, until the mushrooms have softened. Empty the mixture into a sieve and drain well, pressing down with the back of a wooden spoon to extract most of the oil.

In another skillet over medium-high heat, melt the butter. Add the mushroom mixture and blend well. Add the beef gravy and marsala wine. Sprinkle with the parsley, lower the heat to medium, and simmer about 20 minutes.

Preheat the oven to 500°F.

Dredge the meat lightly in the flour. To a third skillet, add the oil to a depth of about 1/2-inch and heat over medium-high heat until just about to start smoking. Cook the meat quickly, about 2 minutes total, turning once. Transfer the meat to a colander and let drain.

Spoon half the mushroom sauce into a 9 x 12-inch baking dish and arrange the beef slices on top. Spoon the remaining sauce over the top of the meat, then place a slice of mozzarella on top of each slice.

Bake 10 to 15 minutes or until it is piping hot and the cheese is melted. Let cool for 5 minutes and serve.

RECIPE

PETER SERVEDIO & MIKE RELLA

peter's meat market

Profile
2344 Arthur Avenue
Bronx, NY 10458
718-367-3136

Peter's is the busy butcher shop located in the Arthur Avenue Retail Market. They sell copious amounts of fresh sausage (cervellata, sweet, hot, fennel, chicken, etc.) and other prepared meats like braciole, veal rollatinis, and flank steak pinwheels and are happy to fill special orders. Essentially, the only meats you won't find here are organ meats and cold cuts—but those are found on either side of Peter's at Mario's Meat Specialties and Mike's Deli, respectively (to avoid competitive poaching within the market).

"As a matter of fact I went to school to become a mechanic.
It was a job with a different kind of grease, that was dark, this is white."
—*Peter Servedio*

Peter's been in the market working at this very butcher shop since he was thirteen, just a few years after his family immigrated from Bari, in 1958. He made the decision to stick with the business after he returned

from a two-year stint in the service during Vietnam. It was 1969, and his ex-boss wanted to go into teaching. Having spent much of his childhood on Arthur Avenue, it was Peter's love for the neighborhood that swayed him to take over the shop. At the time his nephew, Mike Rella, was also working in the store and after a few years he asked Mike to be his partner. Peter explains, "A member of the family, that's the right thing to do. And we've been together ever since."

Peter's the youngest boy, in a family of four boys and four girls. They were all brought over by his father, who'd arrived in the United States in 1955. "I'm the only one in the meat business; the other [boys] were all in construction. I was the only one to get drafted too, and I wasn't even a citizen at the time," recalls Peter, "They made me a citizen once I got out, and I didn't have to pay the $25 fee … but I had an option; I could either go fight or I could go back [to Italy]."

You'll find Peter at the street festivals, like Ferragosto or St. Anthony's, manning spit-roasted pigs and coils upon coils of grilled sausage. His nephew, Mike, is equally visible. "I have to tell you a secret," Mike confides. "All my life I've been here, what would I do at this age? I don't know anything else." It was New Year's Day 1967 when Mike's family joined the rest of his mother's family on Arthur Avenue. His father had been reluctant to leave as he was established with a vineyard and olive cultiva-

Peter Servedio helps a customer at his shop (Peter's Meat Market) while his nephew Mike Rella takes a phone order

tion, but two years of bad weather ruining his crops had convinced him finally to give the States a try. They moved from their farm to a four-room railroad apartment. Mike was thirteen and didn't understand English. After six months his father put him to work after school at the butcher shop with his uncle Pete. He earned $15 a week, and would work before and after school. It was his work at the shop that helped him the most with his English, "They'd say, 'Go get a pail of water.' I used to go get the broom. 'Go get the broom,' I used to go next door and get a coffee. It made me work harder because it was embarrassing." Mike worked straight through school at the butcher shop, while they got by with his mother working at a factory and his father working construction. Mike ultimately graduated from Lehman College in 1976 with a BS in economics, but chose to stay in the business rather than pursue a desire to work at IBM.

His reasoning was logical, "I said let me see . . . I feel comfortable here, I know the people here, I like the people here, I like to mingle with people. I'm good at what I do, so I'll give it a try."

Mike's the current president of Arthur Avenue Retail Market. It's a volunteer position, but it's clear how much care he takes in the role, noting proudly, "Remember without the market here you don't really have a neighborhood, you don't have that flavor that the market possesses. People come here and see the market and go, 'Wow, this reminds me of Europe.' I mean, this was built in 1940. This is like the Yankee Stadium of Arthur Avenue."

BAKED RABBIT

MAKES 4 TO 6 SERVINGS

From:

Peter's Meat Market

peter servedio

Ingredients :

1 3-pound rabbit, cut into 8 pieces
1 tablespoon salt
1 tablespoon ground pepper
1 tablespoon chopped fresh parsley
$1/2$ tablespoon chopped basil leaves
3 tablespoons grated pecorino Romano cheese
6 medium all-purpose potatoes, peeled and quartered
1 cup dry white wine
$1^1/2$ cups chicken broth

Directions:

Preheat the oven to 350° F.

Place the rabbit in a large roasting pan. Sprinkle the salt, pepper, parsley, basil, and cheese on top.

Add the potatoes, white wine, and chicken broth. Bake for 1 hour and 20 minutes.

Peter's family hails from Bari in southern Italy, and according to him this is rabbit cooked "Bari-style."

STUFFED PORK CHOPS
MAKES 4 SERVINGS

From:

Peter's Meat Market

peter servedio

Ingredients:

4 double-cut pork chops
¼ cup bread crumbs
½ pound fresh Italian sausage, diced
1 slice prosciutto, minced
1 slice fresh mozzarella, diced
2 garlic cloves, minced
Pinch of salt and pepper
String for tying
2 tablespoons olive oil
1 cup finely chopped yellow onion
¼ cup butter
1 cup dry white wine

Directions:

Preheat the oven to 350° F.

With a paring knife, cut a pocket in the rounded side of each chop. In a bowl, combine the bread crumbs, sausage, prosciutto, mozzarella, garlic, and salt and pepper. Stuff each chop with the mixture and sew or tie them closed with string.

Heat the oil in a skillet over medium-high heat. When the oil is hot, pat the chops dry then place them in the pan. Brown on both sides, about 3 minutes per side. Remove the pork chops and set them aside in a roasting pan.

Add the onion, butter, white wine, and chicken broth to the skillet. Cook over medium heat, stirring, for 6 to 8 minutes. Add them to the pan with the pork chops and bake for 1 hour. Remove the string before serving, and drizzle the pork chops with the pan juices once plated.

Tips:

Juicy and flavorful, this dish makes a dramatic centerpiece for a Sunday meal. If you're in the neighborhood, Peter sells prestuffed pork chops.

OSSO BUCO

MAKES 4 SERVINGS

From:

Peter's Meat Market

peter servedio

Ingredients :

**4 portions of veal shanks, about 2 $^1/_2$ inches in length,
   each securely tied with butcher's twine or string**
**$^1/_4$ cup (4 tablespoons butter)
   plus 1 to 2 tablespoons butter (optional)**
1 cup finely chopped yellow onion
$^2/_3$ cup finely chopped celery
$^2/_3$ cup finely chopped carrots
1 teaspoon finely chopped garlic
$^1/_2$ cup vegetable oil
Salt and pepper to taste
$^3/_4$ cup all-purpose flour on a plate or wax paper
1 cup dry white wine
1 $^1/_2$ cups beef broth

Tip:

Polenta or risotto are nice accompaniments to this
succulent dish.

Directions:

Preheat the oven to 350°F.

Choose a large, very heavy casserole with a tight-fitting lid. It should be large enough to cook the veal pieces in a single layer. Place the casserole over medium heat and melt the $^1/_4$ cup butter. Add the onion, celery, carrots, and garlic. Cook for 8 to 10 minutes, until the vegetables soften and wilt.

Heat the oil in a skillet over medium-high heat. When the oil is quite hot (test it with a corner of the veal; a moderate sizzle means the heat is just right), season the pieces of veal with salt and pepper, then dredge them in the flour, shaking off any excess. Add the veal to the skillet and brown it on all sides, about 4 to 5 minutes. Place the veal side by side on top of the vegetables in the casserole.

Tip the skillet and draw off nearly all the fat with a spoon. Add the wine and beef broth and heat, stirring, for about 3 minutes, scraping up and loosening any brown bits stuck to the skillet. Pour this liquid over the veal and vegetables. Bake for about 2 $^1/_2$ hours until tender and the meat starts to pull from the bone. You can either serve this dish as is or remove the meat and then reduce the liquid in the casserole over high heat, until the sauce coats the back of a spoon. Add 1 to 2 tablespoons of butter to finish. Remove the string around shanks and reheat gently in sauce before serving.

MEAT&POULTRY

Mario Ribaudo mario's meat specialties

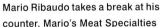

Mario Ribaudo sells organ meats exclusively: tripe, sweetbreads, liver, you name it. Rather unusual in this day and age, but it's a business he's been a part of since he was thirteen years old, working after school from 3 to 11 P.M. at a shop next door to his childhood home—which was down near Veniero's pastry shop in Manhattan. By 1965, a branch of the store opened up in its current location in the Arthur Avenue Retail Market, and Mario bought the owners out in the 1980s. Don't be shy—if you're new to Mario's brand of specialties, he's quick to guide you with an easy recipe suitable for the novice.

Mario Ribaudo takes a break at his counter, Mario's Meat Specialties

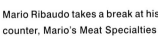

TRIPE

MAKES 6 TO 8 SERVINGS

From:

Mario's Meat Specialties

Adapted from a recipe by Mario Ribaudo

Ingredients:

3 pounds tripe
¹/₂ cup olive oil
¹/₂ cup chopped onion
¹/₂ cup chopped celery
2 garlic cloves, chopped
2 cups Marinara Sauce (page 48)
Grated Romano cheese
Bread or boiled potatoes (optional)

Tip:

Simple is best when it comes to this subtly flavored meat; be sure to buy honeycomb tripe for the most tender results.

Directions:

In a large pot, bring water to a boil. Boil the tripe for 1 hour, adding water when necessary, then drain. Cut the tripe into 1 x 1/2-inch strips. In a large skillet, heat the olive oil over medium-high heat. Add the onion, celery, garlic, and tripe and sauté for 3 to 4 minutes. Add the Marinara Sauce and bring to a boil, stirring occasionally. Reduce the heat to low and simmer for about 15 to 20 minutes. Spoon the tripe and sauce into bowls, sprinkle Romano cheese on top, and serve with slices of crusty bread or boiled potatoes, if desired.

FRIED CALF'S LIVER

MAKES 4 SERVINGS

Ingredients:

4 tablespoons olive oil
1¹/₂ pounds calf's liver, sliced ¹/₂ inch thick
1 cup flour
1 egg, beaten
2 cups bread crumbs seasoned with salt and pepper
1 lemon, quartered
2 tablespoons chopped parsley

Tip:

Liver can become tough if cooked too long, so make sure the sauté pan is hot and keep your eye on the browning time while frying.

Directions:

Heat the olive oil in a skillet over medium-high heat. Dust the liver slices with flour, then dip in the egg and then dredge in the bread crumbs. Fry the liver slices in batches in a single layer until browned, about 2 minutes per side, then drain on paper towels. Serve with lemon, sprinkled with chopped parsley.

SAUTÉED LIVER AND ONION
MAKES 4 SERVINGS

From:

Mario's Meat Specialties
Adapted from a recipe by Mario Ribaudo

Ingredients:

4 tablespoons olive oil
2 large onions, thinly sliced
2 garlic cloves, minced
1 ¹/₂ pounds calf's liver, thinly sliced then cut
   into 1-inch strips
1 cup flour, seasoned with salt and pepper
Salt and pepper to taste
2 tablespoons chopped parsley

Directions:

In a large skillet, heat 2 tablespoons olive oil over medium-high heat. Sauté the onions and garlic until golden brown, about 5 to 7 minutes. Set the onion-garlic mixture aside. Lightly dust the liver pieces with the flour, shaking off any excess. Heat the remaining 2 tablespoons oil in the same pan and sauté the liver, in batches, if necessary, until browned on all sides, about 3 minutes. Return the onions to the pan and reheat. Season with salt and pepper. Serve on a platter sprinkled with the parsley.

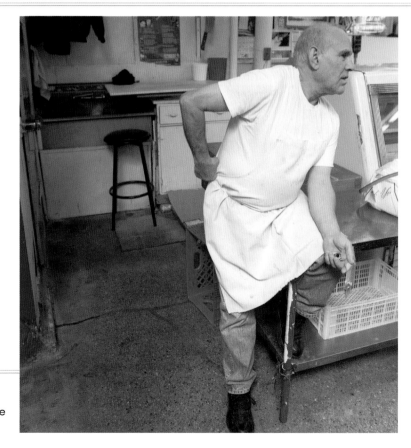

Tip:

Mario adds garlic to his version of this classic home-style recipe.

David Greco of Mike's Deli creates the mother of all sandwiches, hands down.
A version of this sandwich (the Big Mike Combo, which uses provolone instead of mozzarella and leaves out the sopressata) was highlighted in the *New York Times* as one of New York's best sandwiches.
Call him up for specific ingredients if you have trouble finding them — yes, it's worth it.

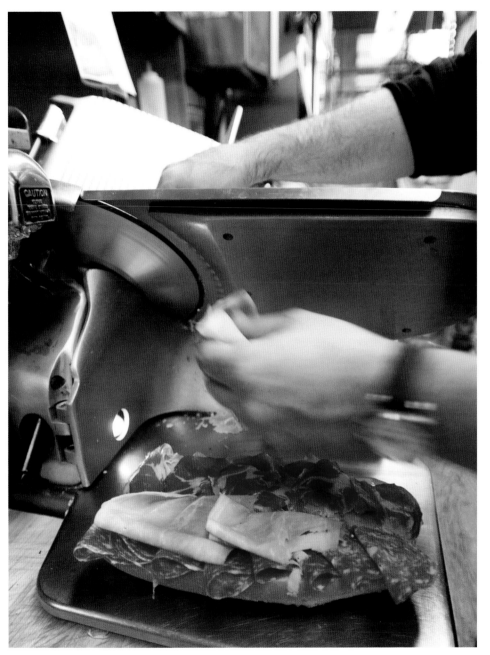

David drizzles reduced balsamic over the final product

THE ARTHUR AVENUE COOKBOOK ANN VOLKWEIN

YANKEE STADIUM BIG BOY
MAKES 1 LARGE SANDWICH

From:

Mike's Deli and Arthur Avenue Caterers
david and his father, michele "pops" greco

Ingredients:

1 Madonia Brothers ciabatta loaf or any hero-size loaf

3 ounces thinly sliced prosciutto

3 ounces thinly sliced Delusso salami

3 ounces thinly sliced San Danieli cappicola

3 ounces thinly sliced San Danieli sopressata

3 ounces thinly sliced mortadella

3 ounces sliced, fresh mozzarella

1 to 2 cups chopped romaine, frise, and red leaf lettuce

$\frac{1}{2}$ roasted red pepper, sliced

Extra-virgin olive oil to drizzle

Reduced balsamic vinegar to drizzle
(simmer 1 cup vinegar until reduced by half)

Direction:

Split the ciabatta and layer the ingredients, drizzling with olive oil and vinegar before serving.

Tip:

To make fresh mozzarella that's been refrigerated taste like it's just been made, submerge the mozzarella in warm water for several minutes, then pour the water out and repeat the process with well-salted warm water. (Of course David claims that Bronx water is the secret to his family's famous mozzarella.)

Sal Biancardi biancardi meats

Biancardi's may be the most full-service butcher shop in the city of New York. They sell a full line of traditional meats—chicken, pork, beef, lamb; they make and cure their own dry sausage, pancetta, and prosciutto; and they make fresh sausages. Specialty meats include baby lamb, baby goat, suckling pig, fresh rabbit, and quail. As Sal points out, "We still bring in the hanging carcasses for the most part, cut everything, break everything down ourselves, so if it's in the animal you can find just about any cut you're looking for."

RIGHT: Sal Biancardi poses in his pristine meat locker. OPPOSITE: Service with a smile at one of the busiest counters on the Avenue

Profile

2350 Arthur Avenue
Bronx, NY 10458
718-733-4058

STROLLING DOWN ARTHUR AVENUE, one of the most artfully designed store windows just happens to be a butcher shop, particularly if your tastes turn toward the seventeenth-century still-life featuring hanging rabbits and slaughtered lambs. Sal Biancardi is part of the fourth generation running the shop. He left currency trading at Morgan Stanley to return to the business, which he describes as, "a whole lot nicer environment." Sal explains that it was a lifestyle decision: "When you grow up in a value-added business like this, where you can see the impact you're having on your customers' lives—the service that you're providing and the product that you're provid-

ing—it's kind of difficult to go into a business where the end result is not the artisanal expertise that you bring, but how much money you make at the end of the day. You know here it's a combination of both. You're definitely bringing some sort of family history into what you do every day. And it's become artistry at this point. With meat cutting it's never really been considered that, but now it's a very skilled labor. It's a dying labor as well. There's not too many people who know how to do it and do it right anymore. So, I guess from that point of view, yeah, the lifestyle is very different, but you see the fruits of your labor on a much more down-to-earth basis."

LEFT: A row of well-worn butcher blocks on a sawdust-strewn floor at Biancardi's. Customers return for the finest meats, cut to order.

Sal's grandfather, Antonio Biancardi, left Naples for the United States in the early 1920s, at the age of thirteen. He eventually opened up a meat store in the Bronx on Morris Avenue. Doing double duty laying tiles while his wife, Anna, ran the store during the day, Antonio was able to bring over, one by one, his entire family, including Sal's great-grandfather. Right before WWII the Biancardis opened the shop on Arthur Avenue. In the 1950s, Antonio died young, of a heart attack. At the time Sal's Uncle Dominick was fighting in Korea and Sal's father, Anthony, was in college, so Anna ran the business by herself for two years until Dominick came back and took over. Dominick died in 2001, and now Sal runs it with his father and brother.

The business appears to be a deep-rooted family tradition, as Sal has traced Biancardis who are still butchers in Naples. He says, "This year is my fortieth birthday and my plans are to go back and try and figure out how this all started and where this all comes from." When asked if he thinks the business will pass to a fifth generation Sal replies, "I was never supposed to be in this business and I wound up in it, so who knows? . . . I have no children myself but I have three nephews and any one of them could take it over. When it has gone so many generations there is a part of you that feels an obligation to continue it. And if the next generation decides not to, then let it be on their watch, not on mine. The business identifies the family, the family is identified with the business, so they go hand in hand."

CHICKEN AND OLIVES
MAKES 4 SERVINGS

From:

Biancardi Meats
sal biancardi

Ingredients:

1 1/2 cups olive oil

One 3 1/2-pound fryer chicken, cut into 8 pieces

Freshly ground black pepper to taste

1/2 cup thinly sliced celery, about 1 stalk

2 garlic cloves, minced

1 1/2 cups dry white wine

3 cups chicken stock (preferably low-sodium)

1 1/2 tablespoons red wine vinegar

15 green Sicilian olives, pitted

2 tablespoons finely chopped thyme leaves,
plus sprigs for garnish

4 tablespoons unsalted butter

Kosher salt to taste

Tip:

If you can't find Sicilian olives, other types can be substituted, but keep in mind that Sicilians are quite large and the amounts should be adjusted accordingly.

Directions:

In a deep skillet or pot large enough to hold the chicken pieces, heat the oil over medium-high heat until just starting to smoke. Pat the chicken dry, season it with pepper, and place it in the hot oil. When the chicken is browned turn it over and brown the other side, about 20 to 30 minutes total, or until cooked through. Set the chicken aside.

Very carefully, as it is very hot, pour out all but 2 tablespoons of the oil. Add the celery and the garlic. Over medium-high heat, lightly brown the garlic but do not burn it, or it will taste bitter. Add the wine, chicken stock, vinegar, olives, and thyme. Raise the heat to high and bring to a boil. Reduce the liquid for 2 to 3 minutes. Add the butter and reduce, about 15 to 30 minutes, adding the chicken back for the last 5 minutes to reheat. Check the sauce for seasoning and adjust with salt, pepper, or vinegar.

Plate the chicken, drizzle with the sauce, and serve, garnished with thyme.

CHICKEN WITH LEMON SAUCE
MAKES 4 SERVINGS

From:

Roberto's Restaurant (see page 120)
roberto paciullo

Ingredients:

4 boneless, skinless chicken breast halves
Flour for dredging
4 tablespoons butter
3 teaspoons grated lemon zest
Juice of $1/2$ lemon
1 teaspoon black pepper
1 cup white wine
2 cups chicken broth
Salt to taste
$1/2$ lemon, sliced
Chopped parsley and basil leaves for garnish

Directions:

With a mallet, pound the chicken breasts until very thin (1/4 inch or less). Dredge the chicken in the flour, shaking off the excess. In 2 large sauté pans set over medium-high heat, melt the butter (2 tablespoons in each pan). Sauté the chicken for 2 minutes, then flip. (You're not looking for it to brown.) Stir in the lemon zest, lemon juice, black pepper, and white wine. Simmer 2 minutes longer. Add the broth and simmer 4 to 5 minutes more. Salt to taste.

Plate the chicken with some of the pan sauce and lemon slices, garnish with the parsley and basil leaves, and serve.

Tip:

This variation of lemon chicken preserves the classic, clean flavors of the dish, and pounding the breasts makes it quick to prepare, yet elegant to present.

SHELL STEAK WITH CHERRY PEPPERS AND BEER SAUCE

MAKES 4 SERVINGS

From:

Roberto's Restaurant

roberto paciullo

Ingredients :

2 shell steaks, bone-in, each 1-inch thick,
   about 2 pounds
2 tablespoons olive oil
2 garlic cloves, slightly crushed
Salt and pepper to taste
1 cup flour for dredging
1 $^1/_2$ tablespoons chopped parsley
$^1/_2$ cup chopped red and yellow cherry peppers
1 cup beer
$^1/_2$ cup crumbled Gorgonzola
$^1/_2$ cup chicken broth
$^1/_4$ cup heavy cream

Directions:

With a smooth mallet, pound the steak until very thin (about 1/4-inch thick). In a large skillet or sauté pan, heat the oil over medium-high heat. Add the garlic cloves and sauté for 1 minute, being careful not to burn them. Season the steaks with salt and pepper, then dredge them in flour, and shake off the excess. Add to the sauté pans. Sauté 4 minutes on each side. Drain off the excess oil.

Add the parsley and peppers and stir with a wooden spoon. Add the beer and stir to deglaze the pan. Add the Gorgonzola and stir into the pan juices, flipping the steaks again. Simmer 2 to 3 minutes. Add the broth. Simmer for another minute and stir in the cream. Re-season with salt and pepper. Serve with the pan sauce drizzled over the top.

Beer, cream, and Gorgonzola conspire in this recipe to create a robust steak sauce.

MEAT & POULTRY

PETER DeLUCA
vincent's meat market

Profile
2374 Arthur Avenue
Bronx, NY 10458
718-295-9577

Vincent's Meat Market is known around the neighborhood for delivering some of the best of the basics. The tidy, efficient storefront occupies a slice of Arthur Avenue between Frank Simeone Square and 187th Sreet, and boasts a long counter stocked with an array of sausages (from hot and sweet to cheese and parsley or peppers and onions) and prime meats. A carving station at the back of the store is a hub of activity, where customers chat with the butcher pounding their veal to order or butterflying their lamb.

The friendly face behind the counter—okay, there are many, but the one greeting the *nonnas* of the neighborhood and asking after the bambinos—is Peter DeLuca, proprietor. When his father, Vincent, passed on in 1979, Peter left college to take over the business—allowing his siblings to collect their law and medical degrees. Heroic, perhaps, but don't think of it as a sacrificial act on his part. He states simply, "First of all . . . my father's name is on my business and I always wanted him to be proud of me. So I worked very hard to build his name. That's mostly why I did this."

Peter Deluca presents a whole lamb

LIKE OTHERS ON THE AVENUE, Peter sees the butcher shop as a "family business" regardless of whether his brothers don the white coat of his trade. The integrity of the market and the legacy are sacred, with openly sentimental ties to Peter's parents, who arrived in this country at seventeen to "make a better life for themselves." Vincent DeLuca got jobs through family friends, trying everything from construction to the leather business. "They would say, 'Come and work over here, you're gonna like it,' but when my father went there," Peter shrugs and chuckles, "he didn't like it." Vincent finally did "like it" when he went to work for a butcher, and he established his first store on 151st Street in 1954. Ten years later he came to the Belmont neighborhood, and Peter moved the market to its current location on Arthur Avenue in 1981.

Peter shares some insights into his business philosophy while conducting a tour of the meat counter. "Here's a top round of veal—look at this, $11.99 a pound, I have people who make stew with that!" he exclaims in mock horror. "Hey, I can't say 'no'—it's their money . . . But as far as business goes, the reason they come here is because they get special treatment. You come to my store, you get what you want. It's not about what we want to give you. And people like that."

One of the advantages to shopping at Vincent's Meat Market is finding wild game and cuts of meat you can't find anywhere else—and you can hardly ever beat the price. Peter beams, "The best stuff comes from Arthur Avenue. I mean, I gotta say it. It's not that I want to be snooty about it or anything but it's the truth. There is no way that you could buy a pound of shell steak anyplace for $8.99 a pound. No way. I know because I don't live here; I live in Briarcliff Manor and you see prime boneless shell for $17 a pound."

Peter grew up in the area, but like most of its former residents, he moved away to raise his family. His childhood memories include the neighborhood's heyday, when Italian immigrants populated the schools and filled Our Lady of Mount Carmel to capacity every Sunday, several times over.

"This was the best neighborhood," Peter says a bit wistfully. "We live in a cul de sac now. My kids never had the upbringing we had. I remember walking down the street with my father, and one of his friends would be sitting on his porch outside, a gallon of wine under his chair. He'd say, "*Vieni*, Vincent; come here, have a glass a wine." You're not gonna see that again. That's it; it's over. It was great; growing up over here was a good thing. And you love your bad times and good times like every place else. 'Cause you go to a better neighborhood doesn't mean it's better. A lot of kids are all screwed up in the head anyway. Over here they have more values. It's more like a family value. You know what I'm saying? Like with my upbringing: Your mother and father was like God to you."

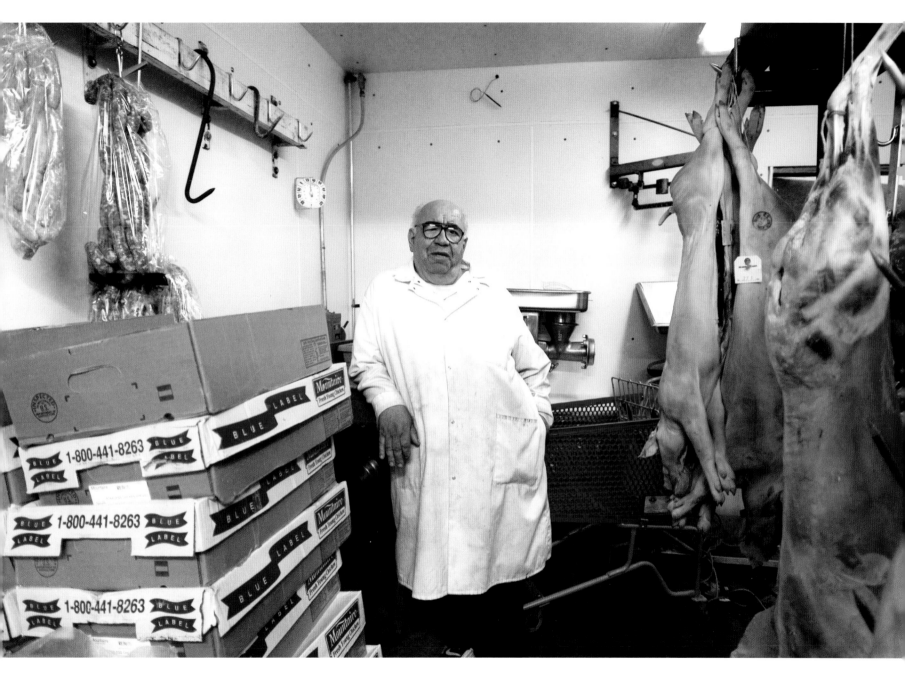

A long-time employee at Vincent's Meat Market

SALTIMBOCCA

MAKES 2 SERVINGS

From:

Vincent's Meat Market

peter deluca

Ingredients :

4 veal escalopes (sliced thin)
Salt and pepper to taste
8 sage leaves (fresh), plus more for garnish
4 slices thin prosciutto
   (double the size of the veal slices)
Flour for dredging
2 tablespoons olive oil
2 tablespoons butter
¹/₄ cup white wine
¹/₄ cup chicken stock
¹/₄ cup Marsala

Tip:

For presentation purposes, be sure to have the prosciutto sliced very thinly for this recipe—the sage leaves should be seen through the transparent slices. A Roman dish, *saltimbocca* means "jump in the mouth."

Directions:

Place veal escalopes between 2 pieces of plastic wrap or baking parchment. Using a meat mallet or a rolling pin, gently beat the escalopes until they are twice their original size and very thin. Lightly season the veal with salt and pepper and place 1 or 2 sage leaves on top (depending on the size). Then cover the veal with a slice of prosciutto that is the same size as the veal.

Secure the prosciutto with toothpicks and lightly dredge in flour, shaking off the excess. Heat the olive oil and butter in a large pan over medium-high heat. Fry the escalopes for 4 to 6 minutes or until golden brown on each side.

After transferring the veal to a serving dish (you can remove the toothpicks at this point), add the wine, stock, and Marsala to the sauté pan and bring to a boil over high heat. Boil until reduced by almost half, about 8 to 10 minutes. Adjust the seasoning and pour the sauce over the veal. Garnish with sage leaves.

ITALIAN SAUSAGE
AND BEAN "CASSEROLE"

MAKES 4 SERVINGS

From:

Vincent's Meat Market

peter deluca

Ingredients:

8 Italian sausages, 2 pounds total

1 tablespoon olive oil

1 large onion, chopped

2 garlic cloves, chopped

1 green bell pepper, seeded and cut into thin strips

8 ounces fresh, skinned tomatoes
  (or one 14-ounce can chopped tomatoes)

2 tablespoons sun-dried tomato paste

One 14-ounce can cannellini beans, drained

Directions:

Preheat the broiler.

Make holes in the sausages using a fork. Cook the sausage under the broiler for about 10 to 12 minutes or until brown, turning once or twice. Heat the oil in a large sauté pan over medium-high heat. Add the onion, garlic, and bell pepper and sauté, stirring occasionally, for 5 minutes or until softened, but the onion and garlic should not be browned. Add the tomatoes to the pan and simmer while stirring occasionally, for about 5 minutes, or until the mixture is slightly reduced and thickened. Stir the sun-dried tomato paste, cannellini beans, and Italian sausages into the mixture and cook for about 4 to 5 minutes. If the mixture becomes too dry, add 4 to 5 tablespoons of water. Transfer the mixture to a serving dish and serve immediately.

Tip:

Peter recommends serving this hearty dish with mashed potatoes or rice.

JOSEPHINE'S WHITE CHICKEN CACCIATORE

MAKES 4 SERVINGS

From:

Catholic Goods Center

John Iazzetti, Jr. (adapted from a recipe by Josephine Iazzetti)

Ingredients :

Olive oil, to cover bottom of deep skillet
One 3 1/2 - pound chicken, cut into 6 to 8 pieces
   (you can substitute any pieces, 6 maximum if
   using only breasts)
1 large onion, chopped
2 cups sliced cremini mushrooms (optional)
1/4 cup dry white wine
1/4 cup chicken broth
2 teaspoons lemon juice or to taste
2 teaspoons white vinegar or to taste
Salt and pepper to taste
2 tablespoons chopped parsley

Tip:

This is an adaptation of John's mother Josephine's recipe, which she has been making since they lived on Arthur Avenue in the 1950s. Serve over linguine or spaghetti.

Directions:

Pour enough olive oil in a deep skillet to cover the bottom and place over medium heat.

When the oil reaches frying temperature, place the chicken pieces in and brown well on both sides, about 10 minutes. Remove the chicken.

Add the onion (and the mushrooms, if you're using them) to the skillet. When the onions are soft (not caramelized), deglaze the pan with the wine.

Add the broth, lemon juice, and white vinegar. (You can use more or less vinegar and lemon juice depending on taste preference.)

Add the chicken back into the skillet, cover and simmer for 20 to 30 minutes. Salt and pepper to taste and garnish with parsley.

RECIPES

Fish & Seafood

Profiles:

Randazzo's Seafood

Roberto's Restaurant

Cosenza's Seafood

BAKED CLAMS

MAKES 2 SERVINGS

From:

Umberto's Clam House

Umberto Ianniello

Ingredients :

12 littleneck clams
1/2 cup toasted bread crumbs
1 tablespoon chopped Italian parsley
1 1/2 teaspoons grated Parmesan cheese
2 teaspoons olive oil
2 teaspoons clam juice

Directions:

Preheat the broiler.

Open the clams, so that they're on the half shell, and set them aside.

Mix all the ingredients except the clams together into a semi-dry paste.

Spoon and pat the bread crumb mixture onto each clam. Place them in a broiler pan and put them under the broiler for 5 to 8 minutes or until the bread crumbs are browned on top.

Umberto Ianniello is proprietor of the renowned Umberto's Clam House in Manhattan's Little Italy, and in 2004 he plans to open an outpost on Arthur Avenue. The Clam House celebrates the recipes and sauces brought to this country by his mother, who hailed from Naples. This recipe is a favorite. "Three generations of our family have been using this same baked clam recipe, unchanged for all these years."

OCTOPUS SALAD

MAKES 8 TO 10 SERVINGS

From:

Mario's Restaurant

Joseph Migliucci

Ingredients:

4 or 5 baby octopuses, about 5 pounds
5 garlic cloves
2 cups finely chopped celery
15 pitted California black olives
1/2 cup olive oil
1/2 to 1/4 cup lemon juice, according to taste
1 teaspoon red pepper flakes
1/3 cup finely chopped parsley
1 tablespoon fresh basil leaves,
    snipped with scissors, or 1 teaspoon dried

Directions:

Have your fish dealer prepare the octopuses for cooking. In a large pot bring water to a boil. Add the octopuses, one or two at a time. When the water returns to a boil remove the octopuses and cool about 5 minutes. Return the octopuses to the boiling water. Let the water return to a boil again and remove the octopuses. Let cool again. Repeat this process once more. Cook the remaining octopuses in the same manner and let cool.

Bring another large pot of water to a boil and add salt to taste. Add the octopuses and simmer 20 to 40 minutes or until tender. When the octopuses are tender, drain them and chill under cold running water.

Cut off and discard any nonfleshy parts of the octopuses if there are any. For example, if the "beak" (a plastic-like small ball) is still in any of the octopuses, remove and discard it.

Cut the octopuses into bite-size pieces. There should be about 5 cups. Place the octopus pieces in a bowl and add the remaining ingredients. Toss to blend and refrigerate 1 hour or longer. Before serving, bring the Octopus Salad closer to room temperature.

Tip:

Forget images of Italian fishermen beating octopuses on rocks to tenderize them; Joseph recommends frequent testing for tenderness as you cook them, since the cooking time will depend on the size and age of the octopuses.

Frank and Joe Randazzo
Randazzo's Seafood

Profile

2327 Arthur Avenue
Bronx, New York 10458
718-367-4139

Randazzo's is as pristine a fish market as you'll find, with imported langoustinos and vongole nestled beside blue crabs, sardines, and pure white Chilean sea bass. At Christmastime eels swim in the tanks in the front of the store, in preparation for the traditional Christmas Eve feast.

PAUSE AT RANDAZZO'S sidewalk raw bar any time of year. Whether you're after the cool bite of a plump oyster in the heat of summer or the jolt of a clam basted in hot sauce on a crisp fall afternoon, Randazzo's never disappoints. Chances are Sinatra will be crooning in the background and one of the Randazzo brothers will be tending the till. Frank and Joe Randazzo are third-generation fishmongers. Their grandfather, also named Frank, left Sicily with his brothers in 1924 and came to America through Ellis Island. Having been fishermen in Italy, it followed that they would open a fish market together. By 1926, their

RIGHT: Customers slurping down oysters and clams at Randazzo's sidewalk raw bar. OPPOSITE: Joe and Frank Randazzo.

grandfather was married. As his grandson Frank now puts it, "They set up pretty quick once they arrived."

Joe and Frank started out helping their father and grandfather run the business by "cleaning the floor and washing down the store every night." Frank elaborates, "The first duty was really just being taken under my father's wing and helping a customer. 'Go get a pound of clams or shrimp,' etc. . . . And we learned the fish business. We started coming, oh, like early high school after school, before that at Christmastime, which is a really busy time for the fish business."

The brothers grew up nearby but not in the neighborhood; however their mother was born in the building right above Dominick's Restaurant. It was the mid-seventies when Frank started spending more time at the store. He says of this time period, "It was alongside my grandfather, my father, my brother, and we all got along well. What happens over the years is you develop relationships with people. It's not you go in, you buy something, you pay, and get out. You chat a little bit, you know a little bit about their family, which people seem to like. Yeah," he smiles, "continuity. I'm young and I've now seen people

I've known and their children, and their children are having children, and they're coming here. It's kind of indicative of the whole area. A lot of the people don't live in the area but they come back to shop."

Plastered on the wall above the cash register are newspaper clippings, Rangers memorabilia, a picture of St. Anthony, and personal snapshots with customers and family. Frank comments on a few of the photographs. "Hillary Clinton came by around 1992 for the first Clinton election; it was like a mob scene. I had never seen anything like that. Matilda Cuomo knew a lot about the fish; she speaks Italian and she's from Brooklyn. Hillary and Donna Hanover not so much." Frank smirks gently and points to a final shot. "This is an old customer here; this guy, he's about at least eighty-five years old, and he used to cut Frank Sinatra's and Mickey Mantle's hair."

LEFT: Oysters at Randazzo's sidewalk raw bar
ABOVE: Frank Randazzo

TURNING TOWARD THE GLISTENING CASES OF SEAFOOD, Frank explains how his brother Joe goes down to the Fulton Fish market every morning and picks the fish. Aside from the Mediterranean fish they import, most of their offerings come from off the coast of Maine, Massachusetts, Maryland, and Virginia, and in the summertime a bit from Long Island and New Jersey. "This year we have the shrimps with the heads. Italians like the fish with heads. Americans like it all filleted. Italians though, like my father says, don't think it tastes like a fish if the head is not on." When asked if there was anything else his father or grandfather taught him about choosing fish for the business Frank modestly summarizes his inherited knowledge. "After a while you can just tell if something's fresh; you don't have to touch it. That just comes over time."

SPECIAL
THICK
BONELESS
BACCALA

BACCALÀ SALAD
MAKES 6 SERVINGS

From:

Randazzo Seafood
Adapted from a recipe by Frank Randazzo

Ingredients:

1 1/2 **pounds baccalà (salt-dried cod fillets; these can be found in Italian, Asian, and Caribbean markets)**
1/4 **cup olive oil**
1/2 **cup chopped parsley**
1/2 **cup pitted roughly chopped black olives**
3 **stalks celery, sliced**
2 **lemons, juiced**
Salt and pepper to taste

Tips:

Baccalà is salt-dried cod, which is reconstituted by being soaked and drained several times before it can be eaten. It's often served as part of the traditional Christmas Eve all-fish dinner. This recipe is a refreshing alternative to the common seafood salad.

Directions:

Soak the baccalà in water for 3 days in the refrigerator to get the salt out, changing the water twice a day. Bring a pot of water to a boil. Add the baccalà and simmer for 15 minutes, then drain. With a slotted spoon, transfer the fish to a bowl and allow to cool at room temperature for 30 minutes. When cool, flake the fish with a fork and gently toss with the olive oil, parsley, olives, celery, lemon juice, and salt and pepper. Chill in the refrigerator for at least 1 hour before serving.

BACCALÀ CASSEROLE
MAKES 4 TO 6 SERVINGS

Ingredients:

1 **pound baccalà**
2 1/2 **to 3 cups Marinara Sauce (page 48)**
1/2 **cup pitted black olives, roughly chopped**
1/4 **cup capers**
1 **medium onion, thinly sliced**

Tip:

Serve this dish warm in a shallow bowl with slices of Pane di Casa (page 142).

Direction:

Soak the baccalà in water for 3 days in the refrigerator to get the salt out, changing the water twice a day.

Preheat the oven to 350° F.

Bring a pot of water to a boil. Add the baccalà and simmer for 15 to 20 minutes, then drain. Flake the fish with a fork. In a 5 1/2 x 8-inch oval casserole dish, combine the flaked fish with the Marinara Sauce, olives, capers, and onion. Bake for 30 minutes.

Both Recipes From:

Randazzo Seafood

Adapted from a recipe by Frank Randazzo

FRIED SARDINES

MAKES 4 SERVINGS

Ingredients:

Olive oil for frying
1 pound sardines
1 cup flour, well seasoned with salt and pepper
Additional salt to taste

Sardines so simply prepared make appearances year-round on the Avenue.

Directions:

Heat the oil in a deep skillet over medium-high heat. Test the temperature by dipping the edge of a sardine in the oil. It's ready if it sizzles. Dredge the sardines in the flour, shaking off the excess. Fry 2 to 3 minutes per side or until golden brown. Remove to a paper towel and sprinkle with salt. Serve immediately.

FRIED EEL

MAKES 4 SERVINGS

Ingredients:

Olive oil for frying
2 eels, skinned, cut into 2-inch pieces
1 cup flour, well seasoned with salt and pepper
Additional salt to taste

Eel is a traditional dish at Christmastime, when you'll find them swimming in the tanks at Randazzo's. Some people like to pickle them, according to Frank. "They fry them then put them in vinegar, oil, hot pepper, and garlic. And serve a few days later." But here he serves them fresh and crispy; he says some people like to cook them with the skin on but he thinks they're more tender when cooked skinned.

Directions:

Heat the oil in a deep skillet over medium-high heat. Test the temperature by dipping a piece of eel in the oil. It's ready if it sizzles. Dredge pieces of the eels in the flour, shaking off the excess. Fry 2 to 3 minutes per side or until golden brown. Remove to a paper towel and sprinkle with salt. Serve immediately.

RED SNAPPER WITH LEMON
MAKES 4 SERVINGS

From:

Randazzo Seafood
Adapted from a recipe by Frank Randazzo

Ingredients:

4 tablespoons olive oil
2 tablespoons chopped garlic
¹⁄₃ cup white wine
2 tablespoons chopped oregano
3 to 4 tablespoons lemon juice
4 red snapper fillets, about 6 ounces each
Salt and pepper to taste
3 tablespoons chopped parsley

Directions:

Preheat oven to 400° F.

Prepare the marinade by combining the olive oil, garlic, white wine, oregano, and lemon juice in a medium-sized bowl.

Place the fillets in a shallow baking dish that's large enough for the fillets to be arranged in one layer (9 x 14 inches). Pour the marinade on top of the fish. Season with salt and pepper and bake for 18 to 20 minutes or until the center is opaque. Sprinkle the parsley on top and serve.

Tip:

This straightforward recipe is lovely served with orzo tossed in garlic and oil and a simple salad.

CRAB SAUCE

MAKES 4 SERVINGS

From:

Randazzo Seafood

Adapted from a recipe by Frank Randazzo

Ingredients:

4 medium blue-claw, hard-shell crabs
(top shell, face portion, and gills removed)
1/4 cup olive oil
4 garlic cloves, crushed
4 cups Marinara Sauce (page 48)
1 pound linguine
1 tablespoon chopped parsley

Directions:

Rinse the crabs and then pat them dry. In a large sauté pan over medium-high heat, heat the olive oil and garlic. Sauté the crabs until the meat turns pale white and is partially cooked, and the claws begin to turn reddish orange, about 8 to 10 minutes. Heat the Marinara Sauce in a large saucepan. Stir 1 tablespoon of the olive oil from the sauté pan into the Marinara Sauce, then place the crabs in the sauce and simmer for 20 minutes. Meanwhile, boil water for the pasta and cook the linguine to al dente. When the sauce is ready remove the crabs and toss the linguine with the sauce and the parsley. Serve the crabs, whole or cut in half, on top of the pasta.

Tips:

Frank enthuses, "Talk to people who make crab sauces—it's one of the best and most flavorful, kind of sweet . . . If you have leftovers, the macaroni [pasta] absorbs the sauce and the oil and the next day it's tasty."

RECIPE

Profile

632 Crescent Avenue

Bronx, NY 10458

718-733-9503

Roberto Paciullo

roberto's restaurant

Roberto's excels in country-style southern Italian dishes, handmade pastas, and an ever-changing lineup of irresistible specials. The setting is a sophisticated melange of farmhouse tables, ochre-colored walls, and velvet curtains.

ROBERTO PACIULLO might serve 240 covers on a given Saturday night—no reservations allowed, but customers are happy to wait for up to 2 hours. It's a testament to the man's talent. Sitting down at one of the restaurant's farmhouse tables for a staff "family" meal (of dry mozzarella grilled with bacon, roasted pepper and olives, fresh tubatini with lobster, and his mother's recipe for wheat cake) one weekday afternoon, he describes his childhood in Salerno: "See, my father [who was a chef], he used to go home every day at one o'clock and cook because we had eleven kids . . . My father, his life was food and sex." Roberto grins mischievously. "I'm sorry to say this but that was it. So he used to go home every day and cook, then after he finished eating he used to put the spoon and the knife and fork on the table like this and he'd say, 'Everything was good

today; what we gonna eat tomorrow?' He used to grab my mother by the hand at two P.M. and go in the bedroom—and this is every day—and come out again six o'clock in the afternoon . . . My house was a feast every day."

And so is his restaurant. Roberto uses all local products, makes his own fresh pasta, and uses nothing from a can—that includes tomatoes, which he purees by hand. Roberto pauses and instructs me to eat the tubatini with a spoon, explaining that it's the way to capture the sauce and "really taste what you're eating. The pasta cooks inside the sauce." It's not unusual for his customers to receive this type of instruction, even with their orders. It's not that he won't give them what they want, he just believes in such standards as everyone at the table ordering something different and having three courses even if you split the first two. Roberto explains, "They get to try a lot of things, that's the way we do it in Italy. We don't go to a restaurant, order a dish of pasta, and say, 'Okay, give me the bill.'"

A relative newcomer, he's had the restaurant on Arthur Avenue for about ten years, and has no plans to leave the neighborhood, which he likens to a small town in Italy. "I got a big proposition to move to [Manhattan], I say, 'Why?' We got twenty-seven in *Zagat* this year, people who read *Zagat*'s they say, 'Oh, where's that? The Bronx?' and everybody benefits."

In the late 1960s, when Roberto was seventeen, his mother's brother brought Roberto to the United States to live. It's not hard to imagine that Roberto must've been a handful for parents with so many children. He explains how his immigration occurred in an offhand manner. "I was the black sheep of my family. I was right in the middle five younger and five older siblings. My mother, she was born here in this country. That's why I could come right over. My uncle, he used to come to eat at my house. And you know when you have a fight with ten puppies there's always one puppy on top of everybody else, you say, 'Oh, we'll take that one,' that's what happened to me. Another espresso?" In response to my enthusiastic "Yes, please," Roberto smiles. "This is fresh espresso. When I go to [Manhattan] and I order an espresso it's no good. 'Wait,' I tell them, 'the owner of this restaurant is not Italian.' He says, 'How do you know?' I say, 'Because if he was Italian from Italy, we're fanatic for coffee, we drink ten espresso a day and if he drinks coffee and he's Italian he would not make coffee like this.'"

A meal at Roberto's is transporting. Just remember: come early, come with a big appetite, and make use of that big spoon.

Roberto mans the stoves in his tiny but hyperefficient kitchen.

CHILEAN SEA BASS WITH CLAMS, MUSSELS, AND TOMATOES

MAKES 2 SERVINGS

From:

Roberto's Resturant

Roberto Paciullo

Ingredients :

3 tablespoons olive oil

3 garlic cloves, crushed

Two 1-inch-thick sea bass steaks

Flour for dredging

2 tablespoons chopped parsley

$^2/_3$ cup dry white wine

4 clams

Salt and pepper to taste

4 tablespoons fresh tomato puree

1 cup clam or fish broth

8 mussels

Directions:

In a large skillet set over medium-high heat, heat the olive oil. Sauté the garlic cloves until lightly browned, about 1 to 2 minutes, then remove.

Dredge the fish lightly in flour, shaking off the excess. Sauté for 1 to 2 minutes on each side, flipping when lightly browned. Drain the excess oil out of the pan.

Add the parsley, wine (away from the flame), clams, and salt and pepper. Sauté 2 minutes longer, then add the tomato puree and broth.

Simmer rapidly (raising heat if necessary) for 4 minutes, then add the mussels. Continue to simmer until all the shellfish have opened (if any are not open 4 minutes after the mussels have been added, discard the unopened ones and remove the fish from the heat). Plate and serve immediately.

The presentation of this dish is striking—dark mussel shells paired with the pristine white flesh of the sea bass.

Joe Cosenza
Cosenza's Seafood

Profile
2354 Arthur Avenue
Bronx, New York 10458
718-364-8510

Joe Cosenza runs his fish store with his son John—a business started by his Sicilian grandfather, who went from stone cutting to fish filleting when he bought out two bickering fishmonger brothers on 187th Street in 1918.

JOE BEGAN WORKING at the store at age thirteen, and is getting ready to retire and leave the store in the hands of his son. John, who began putting his time in at age sixteen, says he always knew he would work at the store, despite his father's wishes that he become a "professional."

"It's a way of living. A lot of hours," says John,

"but it pays off in the long run, plus it's a family business. Gotta keep the tradition."

ABOVE: Cosenza's tempts passersby with the freshest wares from the sea. LEFT: Joe Cosenza. RIGHT: John Cosenza at the oyster bar.

RECIPES

Bread

Profiles:

Madonia Brothers Bakery

Addeo Bakers

Arthur Avenue Bread

CHARLIE LALIMA madonia brothers bakery

Profile

2348 Arthur Avenue

Bronx, NY 10458

718-295-5573

www.madoniabakery.com

In addition to a wide array of cookies and biscuits, Madonia offers the most varied selection of specialty breads on the Avenue, from onion to jalapeño-Cheddar. Try the olive bread; the baker folds the olives into the dough, rather than mixing them in completely, resulting in an airy dough with succulent clumps of chopped olives.

THE NAME MADONIA has been synonymous with quality baked goods since 1918, but to New Yorkers in recent years it has also referred to Mayor Mike Bloomberg's chief of staff. Peter Madonia has taken a step back from the family business while he serves the city, his career of choice. Tragically, Peter's older (and more bakery-inclined) brother, Mario Madonia, died in a car accident in 1988, and Peter took a break from his career in city hall at that time to keep the bakery going. His new partner, Charlie Lalima, has his own story in the bread business, in which he started in junior high school, as a delivery boy in Brooklyn. After years of research working in different bakeries, Charlie eventually built up a large wholesale operation before retiring in 1993. He jokes, "I was

Charlie Lalima, Madonia Brothers Bakery

retired for four months and it was a question of who was going to kill who first, my wife or myself." Serendipitously, a flour merchant pointed Charlie in the direction of Madonia's, and, to the surprise of some of his friends, he began a second career with the small shop.

Charlie is full of such bread-related anecdotes as how a German baker taught him the shelf-life of the Kaiser roll, how Italians stole the bagel business from the Jews, and how they make bread in Toulouse. The row of well-worn bread cookbooks in his office and his insistence on innovation equally express his passion. Soon after joining Peter, Charlie added onion bread, then olive bread, and customers enthusiastically cleared the shelves. The next bread he introduced was the jalapeño bread—pretty far from Madonia's Sicilian roots but a solid recognition of how the neighborhood has changed. Charlie explains, "I know we have a lot of Mexican people in the area so I started making that. Because that's made with cornmeal, jalapeño peppers, Cheddar cheese, onions, and a little garlic. And I'll tell you something: People like that loaf of bread." He even makes a mean Irish soda bread.

His latest creation is a seven-grain cranberry-walnut bread that he says flies out of there on the weekend. He advises his son Adam, who manages the store, "Not everything I try catches on, you gotta change little by little. If you're going to try something don't try it for a few days, try it for a while. You gotta take a beating a little bit if you think something's really going to work." While this marriage of innovation and old Arthur Avenue tradition may go against the grain, the community has accepted Charlie; however, he's sensitive to his status.

"I tell them I'm the new kid on the block. I've been here ten years, but I'm the new kid on the block."

In the end, it's all in the dough for this baker. "I take a cookbook down every day. It's like my wife says, 'He's got a love for it too.' It's what I like to do. I tell my kids that too. I say, 'Do what you like and forget about the monetary value, do what you enjoy and it makes up for everything else.'"

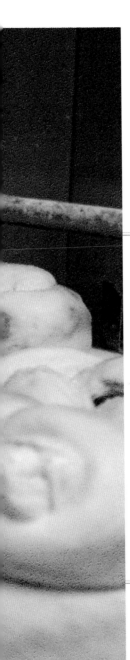

OLIVE CIABATTA
MAKES 2 LOAVES

From:

Madonia Brothers Bakery
Charlie Lalima and Peter Madonia

Sponge Ingredients:

1 cup cool water
1/2 teaspoon dry yeast
(2 teaspoons if using cake yeast)
2 1/4 cups flour

Dough Ingredients:

3/4 cup cool water
1 teaspoon dry yeast (2 teaspoons if using cake yeast)
1 to 2 cups flour (closer to 1 if using bread flour, closer
   to 2 if using all-purpose flour)
1 1/2 cups pitted black olives, roughly chopped
1 teaspoon salt

Charlie is famous for introducing this most sought-after specialty bread to the bakery, an innovation for the neighborhood that came about with Peter's blessing.

Directions:

To make the sponge, in a mixer fitted with a paddle or dough hook and set to medium speed, mix the sponge ingredients until totally blended. It will be a bit soupy. Pour into a bowl, cover with plastic wrap, and let the sponge sit anywhere from 12 to 24 hours. The longer it sits and ferments the better the flavor.

Put the sponge back into the mixer set to medium speed. To make the dough, add the cool water and the dry yeast. Mix for about 2 minutes. Little by little, add 1 to 2 cups of flour. Keep adding flour until the dough begins to pull away from the bowl. You may not need to add all of the flour to reach the proper consistency. The mixing time should total about 15 minutes. You'll end up with a soft, loose dough that is a bit sticky. Mix in the salt only at the end. If you have an instant-read thermometer, it should read about 77° to 80° F.

Sprinkle flour on your counter or "bench." Place the dough on the counter and sprinkle a bit more flour on top. Knead it for a minute, then gently stretch the dough out on the counter, until it forms a rectangle about the size of a sheet pan. Cut the dough into two pieces. Press the dough down gently with your fingers. Cover with a kitchen towel and let sit 1 hour. Sprinkle flour on the top, punch/press dough down with your fingers, and flip it over; cover for 30 minutes more.

Preheat the oven to 475° F.

Press the dough into a rectangle and place 3/4 cup olives along the long edge on the bottom two-thirds of the dough. Fold the dough like a letter (note that they're not mixed into the dough itself). Repeat with the other piece of dough.

Place the dough seam side down and cover. Let rise again for 20 minutes.

Place on a sheet pan and bake for 35 to 45 minutes, possibly as long as an hour. After 35 minutes, test to see if the bottom sounds hollow when tapped. When it does, it's ready. Remove from the oven and let the bread cool to room temperature before slicing.

PANE DI CASA
MAKES 2 SMALL LOAVES

From:

Madonia Brothers Bakery
Charlie Lalima and Peter Madonia

Ingredients:

4 cups flour, plus additional for kneading
1 teaspoon yeast (or 2 teaspoons cake yeast)
14 ounces cool water
$^1/_2$ teaspoon salt (or use 1 espresso spoonful)
Olive oil, for greasing bowl

No Italian-American dinner table would be complete without this country-style bread, perfect for sopping up the gravy. Each of the neighborhood bread bakeries have a version of this loaf. The variations may be slight to the untrained eye and palate, but customers stay loyal to their tradition and "their" bakery.

Directions:

Place 3 1/2 cups flour in a large bowl. Make a well in the middle. Mix the yeast slightly into the flour and slowly add the water until the dough comes together. Add the remaining 1/2 cup flour if the dough is too sticky, but the desired consistency should still be tacky.

Place the dough on a floured "bench" or counter. Add a little more flour and knead for 10 minutes. Use the palm of your hand to stretch it and turn it over.

Spread the dough out slightly and add the salt. Dust with more flour and continue to knead for several minutes. Knead into a smooth ball and let rise for 1 to 2 hours, in a bowl greased with olive oil and covered with a kitchen towel. You'll know it's ready when the dough springs back when you touch it gently with your finger, the temperature of the dough is about 80° F, and it has doubled in size.

Remove the dough from the bowl and cut it in half. Press it down and roll up each piece. Turn them on their sides and roll them up again—this rolls the gas out of them.

Cover the dough for another 30 minutes, this time placed in separate greased bowls; they will double in size once more.

To make the rounds, fold the dough two times, shaping them into balls. Then place the balls seam side down and pull the balls toward you along the counter, being careful not to tear them. The idea is to be forming the dough into smooth balls, gently stretching and pulling the seams to the under side of the loaf each time you pull the balls toward you. Place on a greased sheet pan. Dust with flour. Let sit 30 minutes more, covered.

Preheat the oven to 450° F.

Sprinkle the rounds with flour and press a little air out of the sides. Proof, covered with a kitchen towel, about 10 minutes more. Take a sharp knife and score the top of the rounds several times. Set on another baking sheet and bake for 25 to 30 minutes or until golden brown. Check after 20 minutes. Tap the bottoms and listen to hear if they sound hollow; if they do, they're ready. Remove them and let cool to room temperature before slicing.

SWEET AND SAVORY FOCACCIA

MAKES 2 LOAVES

From:

Madonia Brothers Bakery

Charlie Lalima and Peter Madonia

Sponge Ingredients:

1 cup cool water
1/2 teaspoon dry yeast
  (or 2 teaspoons cake yeast)
2 3/4 cups flour

Dough Ingredients:

1/4 cup cool water
1 teaspoons dry yeast
  (or 2 teaspoons cake yeast)
1 to 2 cups flour (closer to 1 if using bread flour,
  closer to 2 if using all-purpose flour), plus additional
  for kneading
1 teaspoon salt

Sweet Topping Options:

2 figs, sliced, red grapes, banana slices,
plums, sugar and cinnamon

Savory Topping Options:

sliced tomatoes/tomato sauce, sliced onions,
sliced mushrooms, sliced bell pepper, sliced olives,
rosemary and kosher salt, olive oil, to drizzle on top

Tips:

You can make savory appetizers or sweet dessert focaccia
with this recipe. The amounts and exact toppings are flexible, as indicated. Charlie recommends using bottled water
for the most consistent results.

Directions:

To make the sponge, in a mixer fitted with a paddle or dough
hook, at medium speed, mix the sponge ingredients until totally
blended. It will be a bit soupy. Pour into a bowl, cover with plastic
wrap, and let sit anywhere from 12 to 24 hours. The longer it sits
and ferments the better the flavor.

Preheat the oven to 450° F.

To make the dough, place the sponge back into the mixer set
to medium speed. Add the cool water and yeast. Mix for about 2
minutes. Little by little, add 1 to 2 cups of flour. Keep adding the
flour until the dough begins to pull away from the bowl. You may
not need to add all of the flour to reach the proper consistency.
The mixing time should total about 15 minutes. This is a soft, loose
dough that is a bit sticky. Mix in the salt only at the end. If you have
an instant-read thermometer, it should read about 77° to 80° F.

Sprinkle flour on your counter or "bench." Put the dough out
onto the counter and sprinkle a bit more flour on top. Knead for a
minute and make a nice smooth ball. Gently stretch the dough out
on the counter, until it forms a rectangle about the size of a sheet
pan. Cut the dough into two pieces. Re-form into smooth balls and
let them rest for 2 to 3 minutes. The dough is ready if it springs
back when you poke it.

Press it down gently with your fingers into two circles about
8 inches around. Place on a greased sheet pan. Place your desired
toppings on the dough, as you would with a pizza. If you're making
the savory version end with a sprinkle of kosher salt, an herb like
rosemary, and a drizzle of olive oil; on the sweet version, finish
with a sprinkle of sugar and cinnamon.

Bake the focaccia on a sheet pan or a baking stone about 20 minutes total, until nicely browned.

Do not open the oven door until at least 8 minutes have passed,
as the heat escaping will prevent the dough from browning and
crisping properly.

LAURENCE ADDEO, SR.
& LAURENCE ADDEO, JR.

addeo bakers

Come early to get the superb Addeo pane di casa—you never know when they might run out. Other highlights include their bread sticks and seeded semolina. Their friselle and plain biscotti—hard biscuit-like breads—are delicious served under a meat stew or topped with a tomato, basil, and garlic salad.

"IT WAS WRITTEN with a handshake and a kiss," says Laurence Addeo, Sr., of his father Gennaro's start in the bakery business in 1927. A *compara* provided Gennaro, who was a furniture polisher at the time, with the funds to open a bakery in East Harlem with his brother, Thomas. By 1933, they'd moved the business to Belmont, and by 1944 Gennaro opened a bakery in the current Hughes Avenue location. Laurence remembers, "When we had war drives this store was vacant and as kids we would come in here because they were driving for copper and any kind of metal. And the front of the store was used for a depot. We would come in here and rip out all the pipes. Little did I know we would be putting it all back in."

Profile

2372 Hughes Avenue
Bronx, NY 10458
718-367-8316

Laurence Addeo, father and son,
in a room full of family memories

Some of Laurence Senior's fondest memories revolve around the high-ceilinged back room of the bakery, where the industrial carousel ovens anchor the room like vast hearths.

Racks upon racks of freshly baked loaves stand on all sides and a side door opens on to the street. Mrs. Addeo [Vincenza] was famous for her "bottomless pot," which she'd keep on the stove all day long, doling out well-seasoned morsels to anyone who stopped by. "At holidays we'd clear out all those racks and we'd have a long table. We'd have about forty people here," Laurence Senior remembers. "At Thanksgiving people would bring their turkeys in and we'd cook their turkeys free of charge.... The week before Easter my father would go upstate to a place called Marlboro and there he would buy a little lamb or goats for the Easter holiday and he would bring them home and we would play with them down in the basement where he kept them. A couple days before the holidays they were slaughtered and we would never eat them because they were our playmates. We would never eat the lamb."

On this afternoon, the week before Easter, Laurence Senior stands beside his son, Laurence Junior, brushing egg wash on loaf after loaf of Easter bread. Returning customers repeatedly interrupt our conversation, many from far away, making their annual holiday appearance. Laurence Senior gives his son a stern tip on how many to brush before distributing the multicolored sprinkles. With an exaggerated grimace, Laurence Junior com-

ments, "First I swept the floor because he wouldn't let me touch the bread. Then I did the bread sticks and he used to yell at me because I wouldn't do it right. Basically I got criticized by my father all the way up into my thirties." The fireworks between this father and son duo are infamous in the Addeo clan, particularly after Laurence Junior first decided he wanted to work full time at the bakery. Their battles culminated in one big blowout during which Laurence Junior threatened never to return. "It was very dramatic; it happened on Good Friday." Laurence Junior shakes his head. "A lotta fighting, a lotta fighting. I love my father even more because we both have the strength to stand up for what we believe in. And what we believe in is really of common interest but there can only be one person in charge. We're both stubborn and pigheaded but my father has done this a lot longer than I have and knows a lot more about it than I do. He moved to Florida this December. This was the first Christmas in his entire life that he was not in this bakery."

Laurence Senior got his start as a delivery boy. "We would make the deliveries in Harlem by going up to the top of one building and going down another building to save us going up and down. Because they were tenements they were all connected. We had a wicker basket that was filled with the bread and we knew what the customers were taking more or less. We used to leave bread tied on their doorknobs because it was early, you know, five-thirty in the morning." Like for many kids in the neighborhood at the time, the family business came first, before and after school, on holidays. But many old-timers wax poetic over a particular pastime: stickball. Laurence Senior emphasizes the importance of this game among his friends: "The thing about this neighborhood was we had no recreation. It was stickball. We used to use a little red ball called a 'Spaldeen' [a Spalding high-bounce ball], and we would get a broomstick, or whatever we could find that would be discarded. And we would get a team formed and we would play in the middle of the street. Now in those days there were very few automobiles. Come Sunday morning, there'd be two or three cars and we would move them; get in the car and release the brake and push the car. The guy would come, 'Hey, where'd you guys push my car now?' We'd say, 'It's over there around the corner, no need to get excited over it.' Every Sunday we'd have a team but I would be working Saturday night. So, three or four of my friends would come in and help me with the baking so that I would get through. Some of them would come up and sleep with me, some of them would sleep on top of the flour bags. In those days the flour came in cotton bags. It was comfortable. Next day we'd play stickball. My friends would come in after going out until about five in the morning so we could play. Get up at about 8 A.M. Play stickball all day Sunday. And they would do that with no pay just so I could play stickball with them. It became quite a thing. Sometimes we'd have six, seven guys here helping out, all of us getting in each other's way. But it was a lot of fun."

Laurence Junior and his cousin Thomas run the bakery these days, following in their respective fathers' footsteps. Laurence Junior relates, "The only time my uncle [Salvatore] was not in this business was when he was in the service. They lived upstairs. My father and his brother slept in the same bed until they got married. And my aunts all slept in one bed until they got married. My grandmother would sit by the register in a chair and with one eye she'd watch the register and with the other eye she'd be watching to see if her daughters were trying to go out. Our fathers didn't go out, they just worked." Old photographs on the wall read "Panetteria Napolitana"; true to their roots, the family still makes a pane di casa in the Neapolitan-style. "It's just a round light loaf that is basically filling and good for sauces and gravies and stuff like that, because that's how they ate," Laurence Junior explains. "When they said clean the bowl, they really meant clean the bowl. Take the bread, wipe it all out, and eat it, don't leave anything."

Laurence Senior says he really enjoyed his winter in Florida. He hadn't taken more than a couple of weeks off a year up till now, and he's reaping the rewards of his hard work. But you can see the importance of returning, of belonging, as he deftly handles the loaves, chides his son, and greets childhood friends. Pausing for a moment he reflects, "They used to look down on Arthur Avenue. Today, it's something to look up to."

Laurence Addeo, Jr. tells a story, with Laurence Sr.

CHOCOLATE ROLLS

MAKES 12 ROLLS

From:

Addeo Bakers

Laurence Addeo, Jr.

Ingredients:

1¹/₂ packets yeast (3¹/₄ teaspoons)

¹/₂ cup plus 1 teaspoon sugar

3 cups white flour, plus ¹/₄ cup if needed,
   and additional for kneading

1 tablespoon salt

¹/₂ cup cocoa

1 egg yolk

¹/₂ cup dark raisins

¹/₂ cup golden raisins

¹/₂ to ¹/₃ cup chocolate chips

Olive oil (for greasing bowl)

Directions:

Dissolve the yeast in ¹/₂ cup of hot water (about 98°F, just warm enough so that when you put your finger in it, it doesn't quite feel warm or cool) with 1 teaspoon sugar.

Mix the 3 cups flour, salt, cocoa, and the remaining ¹/₂ cup sugar in the bowl of a mixer on stir at low speed. Add the dissolved yeast. Add the egg yolk. Slowly add another cup of water a little at a time until the dough comes together. Add the other ¹/₄ cup of flour, if needed. Increase the speed for 3 minutes. The resulting dough should be tacky but not batter-like.

Reduce the speed and slowly add the raisins and chocolate chips until mixed. Dump the dough onto a floured board and knead gently to make a nice smooth ball. Place in a clean, lightly oiled bowl. Cover with plastic or a clean cloth, place in a warm place, and let rise until doubled, about 1 to 1¹/₂ hours. Slide the dough onto a clean surface and divide into twelve equal pieces (about 3 ounces each). Place on a cookie sheet covered with parchment paper. Dust with flour and cover with plastic. Let proof 30 minutes. Remove the plastic.

Preheat the oven to 400° F.

Bake for 30 to 40 minutes until browned. Let cool on a rack.

Addeo's contributes an innovative favorite, worth both the effort and the calories.

RAISIN NUT ROLLS

MAKES 12 ROLLS

From:

Addeo Bakers

Laurence Addeo, Jr.

Ingredients:

1 ¹/₂ packets yeast (3 ¹/₄ teaspoons)

1 teaspoon sugar

2 ¹/₂ cups white flour, plus additional for kneading

¹/₂ cup whole-wheat flour

2 tablespoons salt

2 tablespoons honey

¹/₂ cup walnuts

¹/₂ cup dark raisins

¹/₂ cup golden raisins

Olive oil (for greasing bowl)

Directions:

Dissolve the yeast in ¹/₄ cup hot water (98° F, just warm enough so that when you put your finger in it, it doesn't quite feel warm or cool) with 1 teaspoon sugar. Make sure it is active and foaming. Mix the flours, salt, and honey in the bowl of a mixer on stir at low speed. Add the dissolved yeast. Slowly add 1 cup of water a little at a time until the dough comes together. Increase the speed for 1 minute. The resulting dough should be tacky but not batter-like. Reduce the speed and slowly add the walnuts and raisins until mixed. Dump the dough on a floured board and knead gently to make a nice smooth ball. Place in a clean, lightly oiled bowl. Cover with plastic or a clean cloth, place in a warm place, and let rise until doubled, about 1 to 1 ¹/₂ hours.

Slide the dough onto a lightly floured surface and cut it into twelve equal pieces. Roll them into smooth balls and place on a cookie sheet covered with parchment paper. Dust with flour and cover with plastic. Let proof 30 minutes.

Preheat the oven to 400° F.

Remove the plastic and bake for 30 minutes until browned and crisp. Cool on a rack.

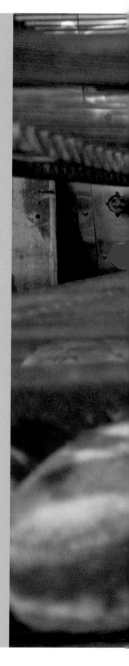

Here's another specialty bread that's a sweet alternative to the average dinner roll.

Laurence Addeo, Jr. manning the carousel ovens

Profile

2344 Arthur Avenue

Bronx, NY 10458

718-365-8860

ARTHUR AVENUE BREAD

A rthur Avenue Bread's 30,000-square-foot factory is by far one of the most far-reaching businesses on the Avenue, delivering bread wholesale to the tristate area. It was started in 1954 by Gerardo and Onorina Galliano, and many of the recipes are a hundred years old, brought intact from a family baking tradition in Avelino, outside Naples. All of their traditional southern Italian breads are still made by hand, but they've added some machine-made rolls and heroes. The year 1982 was a turning point for the family; they suffered a devastating fire at the bakery and the death of their founder, Gerardo. But the Gallianos rebuilt on the same site and have plans for further expansion. Jerry, now the third generation, enjoys being part of his family business:

"I WALK DOWN THE STREET and all these old ladies—I'll be honest, I don't know their names—come up to me and say, 'Hi, Gerardo, how are you?' because I have

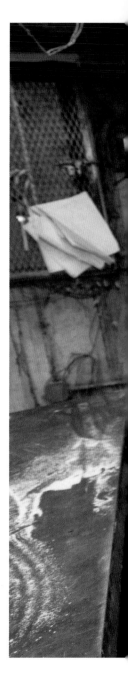

my grandfather's name and they know me from playing across the street in the park when my mother was packing bread. My father was here almost twenty-four hours a day, and my mother was packing and delivering bread pregnant. Sometimes it's stressful, but how could you imagine not breathing, not being part of the bakery? My grandfather, my grandmother, my father, and my mother put their life into this."

It goes beyond bloodlines for Jerry, however, and he emphasizes how the bakery plays a role in the ever-changing ethnic makeup of the neighborhood: "Food unites," he says, "it really does. You should have seen my wedding dinner; it was all these workers, Argentineans, and Hispanic people. We produce bread, but we're one family. We earn our money and we live off this place, a hundred families do because there are a hundred people here. That's what's important at the end of the day, feeding your family."

OPPOSITE: Factory workers from a variety of ethnic backgrounds bake at all hours to fill store counters and displays. "Food unites," says Jerry Galliano of Arthur Avenue Bread.

RECITES

RECIPES

Sweets

Profiles:

Artuso Pastry

DeLillo's Pastry

Egidio's Pastry Shop

Anthony Artuso, Sr., & Anthony Artuso, Jr.

artuso pastry

Profile

670 East 187th Street
Bronx, NY 10458
718-367-2515
www.artusopastry.com

On the corner of East 187th Street and Vincent F. Artuso Sr. Way, Artuso Pastry sells an array of decadent frosted sheet cakes, cannoli, sfogliatelli, lobster tails, éclairs, cookies, zepolli, torrone—you get the picture. These guys are just the people to help capture that classic birthday cake shot and are serious about the tradition of Italian pastries; just witness customers returning home from Artuso's around the holidays, loaded down with string-tied boxes.

THE ARTUSO STORY begins in 1930 when Vincent, Jack, and Anna Artuso immigrated with their family from Calabria, at ages eleven, thirteen, and nine. To help make ends meet, Vincent and Jack built shoeshine boxes, but Vincent wasn't fond of the work and sought out a position washing pots and pans at Belmont's Spagnola Pastry Shop. He was a master sergeant in the kitchen during WWII, and by the end of the war was able to buy Spagnola's with a partner. He eventually bought the partner out and brought his uncle and brother into the business. That was 1946 and Artuso Pastry still occupies the same location—only now the neighboring side street is named for Vincent.

Four generations work for the business, which also has locations in Thornwood (run by Jack's son, Bobby) and Yonkers (currently run by Aunt Anna, the last living founder).

Mount Vernon is now home to the factory for their expanding wholesale business, shepherded by Anthony Artuso, Jr.

Anthony Artuso, Sr., is at the helm of the retail arm. He says it took him seventeen years to take a vacation, and it's not hard to imagine as he takes yet another call regarding the details of a cake order. Soft spoken and modest, Anthony Senior is passionate about preserving the recipes and maintaining the standards, even as they expand the reach of their products. "My son and I are on a mission of sorts to try to preserve the recipes that the old-time bakers have. South American cultures are starting to put their roots into the baking field and naturally they don't have the Italian recipes, but they're learning from Italian bakers. Because when we had a big influx of Albanians a lot of them worked in Italian restaurants and they worked up the ladder the same way the prior immigrant flow did. You know the Germans, the Jews, the Italians, the Irish. Same story, you start at the kitchen sink and you work your way up. And we were talking to this old-time Italian baker saying 'What can we preserve?' He says, 'Really, what *can* you preserve?' And he was right because we know if we tried to make a mix that was here twenty years ago it may not work . . . All these artificial ingredients, protein content, ash content, all of that changes."

The classic pastries at Artuso's don't seem to have suffered from the adjustments to the nuances of modern ingredients. Not only do the Artusos tackle the art of the many-layered sfogliatelli, they succeed in making them on a wholesale level. Anthony Junior

ABOVE: Ladyfingers, nut biscotti, amaretti, and "S" cookies. RIGHT: Anthony Artuso, Jr. and Anthony Artuso, Sr., outside the storefront of Artuso Pastry.

Cannoli, a signature Arthur Avenue pastry
OPPOSITE: "S" cookies, a favorite at weddings

followed his father into the business after obtaining a degree in business management.

He considered real estate and stock trading before deciding to place his efforts here. He explains, "It's the Italian conscience. Everyone's doing it for the next generation but also to reap some of the rewards this time around. The businesses keep us together and what holds the businesses together? The families . . . These guys got together with organizations at the time and provided countless jobs, in fact the city even named a street after my grandfather. They don't do that for knuckleheads, they do that for nice people, not millionaires, not saints, not governors. They do that for people that gave back to the community. We're trying to get the respective streets named after the original owners of the stores, 'cause people who used to shine shoes and couldn't speak English have now changed hundreds if not thousands of lives over the past fifty years. Directly or indirectly that is their contribution to society."

In his unwavering respect for the sacrifices of his past relatives, Anthony Junior echoes the feelings of many of the third- and fourth-generation sons of Arthur Avenue businesses. But he sums up his priorities in a simple statement: "This is deeper than just selling cannoli. You're a part of people's weddings; you're a part of people's celebrations. You're talking about the *cake!*"

ITALIAN RICOTTA CHEESECAKE

MAKES 8 TO 10 SERVINGS

From:

Artuso Pastry

Anthony Artuso, Jr., and Anthony Artuso, Sr.

Pasta Frola (crust) Ingredients:

2 cups all-purpose flour (unbleached),
   plus additional for kneading
1/2 cup sugar
1/4 teaspoon salt
1/2 teaspoon baking powder
1 stick butter (4 ounces), chilled, cut into 8 pieces
2 large egg yolks

Ricotta Filling Ingredients:

1 1/2 pounds whole-milk ricotta
1/3 cup sugar
4 large eggs
1 teaspoon vanilla extract
1 tablespoon anisette
3 tablespoons citron or mixed candied fruit
1/4 teaspoon cinnamon

Artuso's cheesecake is the real deal, less sweet and a bit more subtly flavored than the "New York-style" cream cheese version.

Directions:

To make the crust, combine the flour, sugar, salt, and baking powder in a medium bowl and mix. Add the butter and work it into the flour mixture, like pie dough (this can be done by hand or in food processor), until there are pea-sized pieces of butter. Stir in the egg yolks. The mixture will come together into a ball. Briefly knead the dough, cut in half, and shape into two disks. Wrap the pieces of dough in plastic and refrigerate for at least 30 minutes, or as long as overnight. (You'll only be using one of the disks for the cheesecake bottom crust. You can freeze the second for later use, or cut a lattice top for the cheesecake.)

Sprinkle flour on the table to prevent sticking. Using a rolling pin extend the dough until it is 1/4 inch thick all around.

In order to fill a 9-inch pan with the dough, one method is to use a 10-inch pan to cut the dough, like a cookie cutter. Once cut, lift the dough and fill the pan using your fingers to spread evenly and press the dough against the side of the pan.

Preheat the oven to 350° F.

To make the filling, rub the ricotta through a sieve or pulse until smooth in a food processor. Place the ricotta in a 3-quart bowl and stir in the sugar, then the eggs, one at a time.

Stir in the vanilla, anisette, citron or candied fruit, and cinnamon. Pour the mixture over the crust in the pan. The mixture should just come to the top of the crust. (It's okay if it goes over a little.) Place the lattice pieces on top now if you are opting for that.

Bake at 350° F until the filling is set and the crust is baked through, about 60 minutes. Cool before unmolding.

PIGNOLI COOKIES
MAKES 42 COOKIES

From:

Artuso Pastry

Anthony Artuso, Jr., and Anthony Artuso, Sr.

Ingredients:

1 cup almond or macaroon paste (10 ounces)
3/4 cup sugar
1/2 teaspoon vanilla extract
3 large egg whites
1 cup pignoli (pine) nuts

Directions:

Preheat the oven to 325° F.

In a large bowl, cream together the paste, sugar, and vanilla. Add the egg whites (one at a time) and blend until creamy.

Drop the batter by teaspoonfuls onto a lightly greased baking sheet. Top with nuts. Bake 18 to 20 minutes or until golden. Gently remove from baking sheet before cooling as they have a tendency to stick. These are delicious straight out of the oven.

Tip:

The pignoli cookie is yet another southern Italian favorite. Make sure when you buy the almond paste that you're not purchasing marzipan, which has added sugar and will ruin the cookie's soft, slightly chewy consistency.

ANISETTE BISCUITS

MAKES 60 BISCUITS

From:

Artuso Pastry

Anthony Artuso, Jr., and Anthony Artuso, Sr.

Ingredients:

1 cup sugar
3 cups bread flour
1 tablespoon baking powder
$1/2$ teaspoon anise seed (optional)
1 cup Crisco shortening
3 fresh eggs
2 teaspoons vanilla extract
$1/2$ teaspoon anisette oil (available in health food
   stores, or use extract found in a grocery spice rack)

Directions:

Preheat the oven to 350° F.

Mix all the dry ingredients, including the anise seed for those who decide to use it, together in the bowl of a mixer. Add the Crisco and mix until dispersed in the flour. Then add the rest of the ingredients and blend for about 3 minutes at medium speed. Deposit the ingredients into a pastry bag. Using two cookie sheets, squeeze out (or form with your hands if not using a pastry bag), two even lines/loaves lengthwise, about $1^1/_2$ inches wide and 12 inches long.

Bake for 30 minutes, until golden brown. Cool 5 minutes then gently move to a cutting board. Cut $^3/_4$-inch-thick slices. Lay them back onto the sheet pans, return pans to 350° oven, and toast, 20 minutes, until very crisp and deeply golden brown.

Tip:

If you prefer a stronger anise flavor in these wonderfully tender biscotti, you can add the optional anise seed to this recipe.

Emanuela Florio
DeLillo's Pastry

E manuela Florio has been working at DeLillo's for nineteen years, when her brother-in-law Luigi, who was the head baker, took over for the DeLillo family. She met her husband after immigrating to this country from the Amalfi coast in the 1960s; it was a neighborhood romance strictly watched over by their families. "Nine o'clock you had to be in," she remembers. "You were late five minutes, you got whacked."

TODAY EMANUELA works alongside her daughter, Giuseppina, and her twin sons Salvatore, Jr., and Anthony. Stop in for an Italian ice and some of the best pastries in the neighborhood, including lobster tails, cannolis, tiramisu, and éclairs.

Profile
606 East 187th Street
Bronx, NY 10458
718-367-8198

Dominick's Restaurant

Profile
2335 Arthur Avenue
Bronx, New York 10458

Dominick's sets out tables on the Avenue during August's Ferragosto festival. This landmark establishment, bedecked in '70s-era wood paneling and orange tablecloths, is a favorite for family-style, garlic-and-red-sauce Sunday dinners. They don't provide a menu, so tell them what you feel like and go with the flow—from stuffed artichokes to seafood linguine. After espresso, order up some sweet black sambuca. It's a common practice at Dominick's—as evidenced by the row of blue and white bottles behind the bar. Once they've set the licorice-flavored after-dinner drink on the table, you may just find you have a new favorite *dolce.*

Dominick's customers and staff enjoy the warm sunshine during the mid-August Ferragosto Festival. The Avenue is closed to traffic to make room for sidewalk tables and grills boasting spit-roasted pigs and coils upon coils of fresh sausage.

NUT BISCOTTI
MAKES 20 TO 22 BISCOTTI

From:

Addeo Bakers
Laurence Addeo, Jr.

Ingredients:

2 cups flour
²/3 cup sugar
2 teaspoons baking powder
1 tablespoon hazelnut or pistachio paste
3 tablespoons rum
1 tablespoon vanilla extract
2 large eggs
1 cup nuts (hazelnut or pistachio)

Directions:

Preheat the oven to 400° F.

Mix the flour, sugar, baking powder, paste, rum, and vanilla in the bowl of a mixer on low speed, until it becomes coarse and raggy, like pie dough.

Add the eggs and mix until the dough comes together. Then, using your hands, fold or knead the nuts into the dough until fairly evenly incorporated.

Place the dough on a floured board and roll into a log, about 2 x 16 inches long.

Remove to a cookie sheet covered with parchment paper and flatten into a half moon shape (when viewed from the ends).

Bake for 30 minutes until golden brown. Cool slightly, about 5 minutes. Lower the oven to 350° F. Slice the log on a bias into 3/4-inch slices, about 20 to 22 pieces.

Lay the pieces back onto the cookie sheet, cut side down, and toast in the oven for another 20 minutes until deeply golden brown and very crisp.

Tip:

This is the classic hard, crunchy cookie that is best when dipped in a dark espresso.

LADYFINGERS

MAKES 72 COOKIES

From:

Madonia Brothers Bakery

Charlie Lalima

Ingredients:

1 cup plus 2 tablespoons sugar
Pinch of salt
5 large eggs, whole
2 cups sifted all-purpose flour
  (sifted twice, then measured)
1 teaspoon cinnamon, lemon, or orange extract

Directions:

Preheat the oven to 350° F.

Sift together the sugar and salt. In a mixer with a whisk, whip the sugar, salt, and eggs on high speed, until triple in volume and very pale yellow. Fold in the flour and flavoring.

Line a sheet pan with parchment. Place the batter in a piping bag fitted with a plain, medium-size tip (or use a resealable or plastic bag by cutting off the corner to create a small hole). Pipe out small (3-inch-long) bars, about 1 1/2 to 2 inches apart.

Bake for 12 to 14 minutes, until the edges are just barely brown, let cool on a rack.

Tips:

A rather crisp version of this style of cookie, these are easily made into a tiramisu and are also great for dipping in espresso.

"S" COOKIES

MAKES ABOUT 74 COOKIES

From:

Madonia Brothers Bakery

Charlie Lalima

Ingredients:

- 1 cup plus 2 tablespoons sugar
- 1 stick butter (4 ounces)
- 1/2 cup shortening (or use 1 additional stick butter)
- 1/4 cup milk
- 2 large eggs
- 1 tablespoon honey
- 1 teaspoon cinnamon, lemon, or orange extract
- 4 1/2 cups all-purpose flour
- Colored sprinkles (optional)

Tips:

"S" cookies (shaped like the letter) make frequent appearances on Italian wedding cookie "cakes," which tower high with firm biscotti making the base, and a variety of cookies such as anisette, amaretti, sesame, and "S," reaching upward, fashioned together with confectioners' sugar icing and studded with white and green sugar-coated almonds. Ribbon streamers and flowers crown the cake. At southern Italian weddings, before the guests eat the cookies they dance the tarantella around the table. If you're a chocoholic, try dipping these in melted dark chocolate after they've cooled.

Direction:

Preheat the oven to 375° F.

Cream together the sugar and butter and/or shortening. Add the milk, eggs, honey, and flavoring. Gradually add in the flour. Shape the dough into a disk, wrap in plastic, and chill for about 1 hour. Take a small piece of dough (a few tablespoons) and roll it into a small log, about 3 1/2 inches long and 1/2-inch wide. Gently push the dough into an "S" shape. Repeat until all of the dough has been used.

Place the cookies on a sheet pan lined with parchment, about 1 1/2 inches apart. Sprinkle lightly with colored sprinkles (optional). Bake for 18 minutes, until golden brown. Remove and let cool before serving.

AMARETTI

MAKES 76 COOKIES

From:

Madonia Brothers Bakery

Adapted from a recipe by Charlie Lalima

Ingredients:

1 pound almond paste
1/8 teaspoon salt
1 cup granulated sugar
1 cup plus 1 tablespoon confectioners' sugar
4 large egg whites

Directions:

Preheat the oven to 375° F.

Place the almond paste in the bowl of a mixer fitted with a paddle and beat it on medium speed to break up and soften the paste. Add the salt and granulated sugar. Beat on medium speed for about 5 minutes to "cream" it and take away the granularity of the sugar. Add in the confectioners' sugar a little at a time and mix thoroughly. Then add the egg whites, one at a time, until fully incorporated. It should look like a thick batter, not a cookie dough.

Scoop the batter into a pastry bag with a medium to large plain tip. Line a sheet pan with parchment. Pipe the batter onto the parchment, in 1 1/2-inch disks. (You can space them about 1 inch apart, as these cookies do not spread much.) Alternatively, you may spoon them on instead, taking a tablespoon-size soup spoon and scraping the batter from the spoon onto the parchment with a second spoon. This works fine though the cookie will have a less smooth surface. Bake for 12 to 15 minutes or until golden.

Let them cool on the pan for 5 minutes. Then, lift the corner of the parchment and carefully pour about 1/4 cup of water underneath the parchment (between the sheet pan and the parchment). You can tip the pan so that the water runs to all parts of the pan, then let it sit and cool another 5 or 10 minutes. This allows you to release the cookie, which is still moist in the middle, from the parchment, instead of tearing the bottom off. Just be sure the water stays under the parchment and not on the baked cookie.

Tip:

Simple, but moist and full of flavor, this cookie is a classic —see Artuso's Pignoli Cookies (page 168) for a version of this with pine nuts.

Profile

622 East 187ᵗʰ Street

Bronx, NY 10458

718-295-6077

Egidio's Pastry Shop

L ocated at the corner of 187th Street and Hughes Avenue, Egidio's Pastry Shop displays a tantalizing array of cakes in its window. The marble tiles, curving Italian-style pastry cases, and pressed-tin ceiling make it a pleasant stop for a cappuccino (with a dollop of heavy whipped cream) and of Carmela's too-precious-to-eat mini pastries. She insists, "It has to first appeal to your eye." The taste buds won't be disappointed either. Highlights include: mont noirs, chocolate rings, banana éclairs, rialto bridges, cream puffs, and Italian Napoleans (made from sponge cake). Be sure to look for special baked treats like zeppole and sfingi around the feast days.

CANNOLI
MAKES ABOUT 20 CANNOLI

From:

Gino's Pastry Shop
Jerome Reguso

Cannoli Shell Ingredients:

Oil for deep frying
2 cups cake flour
1 cup all-purpose flour
1/4 cup sugar
4 ounces lard (1 stick or 8 tablespoons)
1 tablespoon rum
1 tablespoon honey
Pinch of salt
1/2 teaspoon cinnamon
1 large egg plus egg wash
   (2 eggs whisked with 2 tablespoons water)

Ricotta Filling:

1 pound dry ricotta (impastata), or buy good-quality
   ricotta, line a strainer with cheese cloth, place the
   cheese in it, and drain overnight or a full day
1/2 cup granulated sugar
1/4 teaspoon cinnamon oil or ground cinnamon
1/4 cup mini chocolate chips
Confectioners' sugar for dusting

Tip:

Jerome's (now-deceased) father, Gino, opened his pastry shop in 1961 after working for several years at DeLillo's, located farther down 187th Street. You can order cannoli cutters and rods (sometimes called tubes) online; try Amazon's baking section or specialty baking stores.

Directions:

Heat a deep fryer to 320° F.

In a mixer, combine all the cannoli shell ingredients except the egg wash, adding enough water (1 to 2 tablespoons cold water) until it reaches a doughlike consistency. The amount of water will vary according to the outside temperature/humidity. Roll the dough to the thickness of pasta (1/4 inch). Using a cannoli cutter (an oval-shaped cookie cutter), cut out the cannoli. Place the cannoli ovals in a row and place a cannoli rod down the center. Flip the cannoli up and over, sealing the opposite edges where they meet with egg wash and pressing down.

Deep fry them for 3 minutes, until golden brown.

Combine all the filling ingredients. Let the cannoli shells cool, then using a large-tip pastry bag, pipe the ricotta mixture into the cannoli.

Serve, sprinkled with confectioners' sugar.

THE ARTHUR AVENUE COOKBOOK ANN VOLKWEIN

Visiting Arthur Avenue

In general, the restaurants, cafés, and pastry shops are the only places open on Sundays. The busiest days are Fridays and Saturdays when former residents and foodies make their shopping pilgrimages. Call ahead to confirm hours. The official neighborhood website is: www.the reallittleitaly.com. Check there for feast and festival dates: The Feast of St. Anthony is in June, Our Lady of Mount Carmel is in July, and Ferragosto is in August.

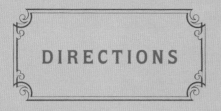
Getting There by Car

From the east or west take the Bruckner Expressway or Cross Bronx Expressway (I-278) to the Bronx River Parkway, North, to Exit 7W (Fordham Road). The Bronx Zoo will be on your left. Stay to the left and go under the overpass and turn onto Arthur Avenue after the traffic light.

From the north take Sprainbrook Parkway that becomes the Bronx River Parkway south to Fordham Road. The Bronx Zoo will be on your left. Stay to the left and go under the overpass and turn onto Arthur Avenue after the traffic light.

Parking can be found on the side streets, but there is a lot on the Avenue across from Mario's Restaurant as well.

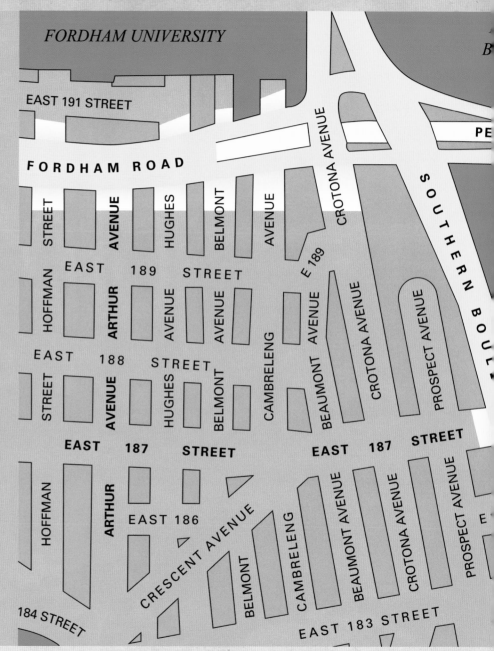

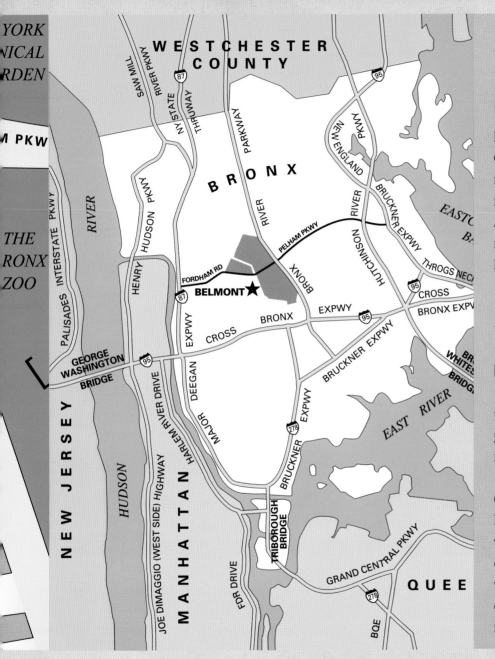

Getting There by Train

One of the most efficient ways to get there if you do not own a car is to take the Metro North Harlem River Line to Fordham Road. Trains run regularly from Grand Central Station and it takes about 20 minutes to reach Fordham Road. From there you can either walk a few blocks east up Fordham Road until you reach Arthur Avenue, where you will walk south to 187th Street, or you may catch the seasonal shuttle bus to Belmont and the Bronx Zoo.

Getting There by Subway

Take the number 4 or D train to Fordham Road then the number 12 bus heading east, getting off at Arthur Avenue. Alternatively, take the number 2 or number 5 train to Pelham Parkway, then the number 12 bus heading west, getting off at Arthur Avenue.

Between shopping and eating, visit the Enrico Fermi Cultural Center (the library) at 610 East 186th Street, housed on the site of what was formerly Cinelli's Savoy movie theater (nicknamed "The Dumps"), where older residents remember watching double features and westerns as children. Today, performances and lectures complement the substantial collection of Italian heritage reference books that the library maintains.

Bread Bakeries

Addeo Bakers (see page 146)

Superior pane di case, bread sticks, biscuits, and more; there's a second location on the same block as the Arthur Avenue Retail Market

2372 Hughes Avenue, Bronx, NY 10458

718-367-8316

Arthur Avenue Bread (see page 154)

Cookies, pane di casa, and more found inside the Arthur Avenue Retail Market or at their main bakery on the Avenue, just above 187th Street

Arthur Avenue Retail Market

2344 Arthur Avenue, Bronx, NY 10458

718-365-8860

Madonia Brothers Bakery (see page 136)

Specialty breads such as olive, onion, and jalapeño Cheddar as well as an abundant supply of cookies, biscuits, and classic breads like ciabatta

2348 Arthur Avenue, Bronx, NY 10458

718-295-5573

www.madoniabakery.com

Terranova Bakery

Pizza bread, bread sticks, basic home-style Italian selections, ravioli

535 East 187th Street, Bronx, NY 10458

718-367-6985

Butchers & Sausage Makers

Biancardi Meats (see page 88)

A full-service butcher shop, from wild game to the basics

2350 Arthur Avenue, Bronx, NY 10458

718-733-4058

Calabria Pork Store (see page 68)

Hot and sweet sopressata, cappicola, and fresh and dried sausage plus prosciutto, bacon

2338 Arthur Avenue, Bronx, NY 10458

718-367-5145

D'Auria Pork Store

Sopressata and dried sausage, hot and sweet, old-style

652 East 187th Street, Bronx, NY 10458

718-584-1040

Mario's Meat Specialties (see page 80)

Specializing in organ meats, from tripe to liver to sweetbreads

Arthur Avenue Retail Market

2344 Arthur Avenue, Bronx, NY 10458

Peter's Meat Market (see page 72)

Wide range of prepared meats and fresh sausage, plus a full range of standard cuts

Arthur Avenue Retail Market

2344 Arthur Avenue, Bronx, NY 10458

718-367-3136

Vincent's Meat Market (see page 96)

Prime cuts, wild game, and the best of the basics

2374 Arthur Avenue, Bronx, NY 10458

718-295-9577

Coffee & Wine

Cerini Gifts

Ceramics, housewares, gifts, and fresh-roasted coffee

662 East 187th Street, Bronx, NY 10458

718-584-3449

Marie's Roasted Coffee

Roasted coffee and espresso beans, china, crystal housewares, and basic gift items

2378 Arthur Avenue, Bronx, NY 10458

718-295-0514

Mount Carmel Wine

Far-reaching selection of Italian wines plus great deals on all wine regions

612 East 187th Street, Bronx, NY 10458

718-367-7833

Delis, Cheese & Imported Goods

Calandra's Cheese

Everything from fresh ricotta to taleggio

2314 Arthur Avenue, Bronx, NY 10458

718-365-7572

Casa della Mozzarella (see page 28)

Sinfully good, freshly made mozzarella, imported cheeses, antipasti, anchovies, pantry items

604 East 187th Street, Bronx, NY 10458

718-364-3867

Joe's Italian Deli

A basic deli with a superior selection of imported goods, particularly olive oils, just ask Joe's wife Marie for guidance

685 East 187th Street, Bronx, NY 10458

718-367-7979

Mike's Deli & Arthur Avenue Caterers (see page 18)

A full-service deli and caterer specializing in antipasti, outstanding sandwiches and panini, imported meats, dried sausages, cheeses, olives, and homemade fresh and smoked mozzarella; table service also available

Arthur Avenue Retail Market

2344 Arthur Avenue, Bronx, NY 10458

718-295-5033

www.arthuravenue.com

Nick's Variety Place

Pots, pans, ceramics, imported cooking and baking equipment

Arthur Avenue Retail Market

2344 Arthur Avenue, Bronx, NY 10458

718-367-7433

Tino's Delicatessen

Basic deli fare from cold cuts to dried sausages, imported pantry items

609 East 187th Street, Bronx, NY 10458

718-733-9879

Teitel Brothers (see page 36)

Huge selection of imported canned goods, seasonings, olives, olive oils, dried legumes and mushrooms, sardines and anchovies

2372 Arthur Avenue, Bronx, NY 10458

718-733-9400

http://www.teitelbros.com

Fish Markets

Cosenza's Fish Market (see page 128)

Broad range of fish, shellfish, cuttlefish, you name it

2354 Arthur Avenue, Bronx, New York 10458

718-364-8510

Randazzo's Seafood (see page 110)

All the standards plus numerous imported fish, lobster, shellfish, and eel at Christmastime

2327 Arthur Avenue, Bronx, New York 10458

718-367-4139

Fresh Pasta

Borgatti's Ravioli & Egg Noodles

(see page 42)

Fresh pasta cut to order and two types of ravioli—spinach and meat and cheese

632 East 187th Street, Bronx, NY 10458

718-367-3799

Pastry Shops

Artuso Pastry (see page 162)

Tremendous selection of birthday cakes, pastries, cookies, and cannoli

670 East 187th Street, Bronx, NY 10458

718-367-2515

www.artusopastry.com

DeLillo's Pastry Shop (see page 170)

Excellent variety of the larger classic pastries, cookies, gelato

606 East 187th Street, Bronx, NY 10458

718-367-8198

Egidio Pastry Shop (see page 178)

Eye-catching array of mini pastries and cakes, espresso bar

622 East 187th Street, Bronx, NY 10458

718-295-6077

Gino's Pastry Shop

Specializing in wedding cakes, zeppole, cookies

580 East 187th Street, Bronx, NY 10458

718-584-3558

Produce Vendors

Boiano's Fruit

Large range of fresh vegetables and fruit

Arthur Avenue Retail Market

2344 Arthur Avenue, Bronx, NY 10458

718-220-0346

Joe's Garden of Plenty

Seeds, seasonal vegetables, potted herbs, plants

Arthur Avenue Retail Market

2344 Arthur Avenue, Bronx, NY 10458

718-733-7690

Restaurants & Cafés

Ann & Tony's

Italian-American Neapolitan fare, four generations strong, catering available

2407 Arthur Avenue, Bronx, New York 10458

718-933-1469

Arthur Avenue Café and Focacciaria

Classic panini, antipasti, dolci, and more, plus live music on the weekends (and it's run by David Greco's mom, Antoinette)

2329 Arthur Avenue, Bronx, New York 10458

718-562-0129

www.arthureavenue.com

Dominick's Restaurant

A casual, landmark restaurant, family-style tables, great seafood linguine

2335 Arthur Avenue, Bronx, New York 10458

718-733-2807

Emilia's Restaurant

Classic Sicilian Italian-American fare

2331 Arthur Avenue, Bronx, New York 10458

718-337-5915

Enzo's Café

Espresso, desserts

2339 Arthur Avenue, Bronx, NY 10458

718-733-2455

Full Moon Pizzeria

Great pizza, a selection of hot heroes, homemade soups

600 East 187th Street, Bronx, NY 10458

718-584-3451

GianTina Ristorante

Local favorite, same family as Full Moon, pleasant staff, full menu

602 East 187th Street, Bronx, NY 10458

718-933-2800

Giovanni's Restaurant

Specializing in brick oven pizza, pastas

2343 Arthur Avenue, Bronx, NY 10458

718-933-4141

Mario's Restaurant (see page 52)

Noted for its Neapolitan dishes, pizza—a landmark

2342 Arthur Avenue, Bronx, NY 10458

718-584-1188

Pasquale's Rigoletto

Large, well-known restaurant serving classic Italian-American dishes

2311 Arthur Avenue, Bronx, NY 10458

718-365-6644

Roberto's Restaurant (see page 120)

Fresh pastas, everything from veal to bass cooked to perfection—Italian, not Italian-American

632 Crescent Avenue, Bronx, NY 10458

718-733-9503

Umberto's Clam House (see page 107)

A new offshoot of Umberto's Clam House in Manhattan's Little Italy

2356 Arthur Avenue, Bronx, NY 10458

INDEX